JENNY HOLZER

JENNY HOLZER

Diane Waldman

GUGGENHEIM MUSEUM

ISBN 0-8109-6892-4 (hardcover, Abrams)
ISBN 1-85437-206-8 (hardcover, Tate)
ISBN 0-89207-184-2 (softcover)

Printed in Germany by Cantz

Designed by Cara Galowitz

Hardcover edition distributed in
the United States and Canada by
Harry N. Abrams, Inc.
100 Fifth Avenue
New York, New York 10011

Hardcover edition distributed in
the United Kingdom, Eire, and Europe by
Tate Publishing
Millbank
London SW1P 4RG

Published by
Guggenheim Museum Publications
1071 Fifth Avenue
New York, New York 10128

Jenny Holzer
Solomon R. Guggenheim Museum
December 12, 1989–February 25, 1990

This exhibition was supported in part by
generous funds from Jay Chiat and the
National Endowment for the Arts.
Additional assistance was provided by
The Owen Cheatham Foundation,
The Merrill G. and Emita E. Hastings
Foundation, the New York State Council
on the Arts, and anonymous donors.

Front cover: From the *Survival* series.
Daktronics double-sided electronic sign,
20 x 40 feet. Installation, Caesars Palace,
Las Vegas, 1986. Organized by Nevada
Institute of Contemporary Art, University of
Nevada, Las Vegas.

Back cover: From *Arno*. Kodaclit-film xenon
projection, approximately 200 x 115 feet.
Installation, part of a collaborative project
with Helmut Lang, Palazzo Bargagli,
Florence, 1996. Organized by Biennale di
Firenze, Florence.

CONTENTS

opposite and pages 10–11:
From *Truisms, Inflammatory
Essays,* and the *Living* series.
Bethel White granite
benches and LED sign;
benches: 17 x 36 x 18 inches
each; sign: 14 inches x
530 feet 9 ½ inches x
4 inches. Installation,
Solomon R. Guggenheim
Museum, New York,
1989–90.

THE SENSES
LEAVE THE FAMILY
FORGET THE DEAD
LIMIT TIME
OBJECTS
FORGET TRUTHS

In retrospect, Jenny Holzer's 1989–90 exhibition at the Solomon R. Guggenheim Museum can be seen as a watershed event in her career, for it gave the artist both an opportunity to work on a larger scale than ever before and the ability to reach a much broader audience. Her success in New York was almost immediately followed by a triumphant showing at the 1990 Venice *Biennale*, where her installation at the American Pavilion (a venue owned and operated by the Solomon R. Guggenheim Foundation) was awarded the Leone d'Oro prize for the best pavilion.

Every visitor to Holzer's exhibition at the Guggenheim remembers the spectacular LED sign that wound up the spiraling ramp of the Frank Lloyd Wright building. Because this site-specific work was not unveiled until the exhibition's opening, it could not be photographed in time for the catalogue that accompanied the show. This inherent inadequacy, coupled with the fact that the book sold out quickly, created the need for a second edition. Work has proceeded on this revised edition for more than three years, during which time the book has been completely redesigned and rethought. It now includes many of the artist's achievements since the Guggenheim show, such as the *Biennale* installation, her *Lustmord* series (based on atrocities in Bosnia), and major installations in Japan, Germany, and, most recently, at the 1996 Florence *Biennale*. Holzer has worked closely with the Guggenheim to make this a book that charts her entire career. Generously, she has agreed to include in it all of her writings to date.

The publication of this book coincides with a new aspect of the Guggenheim's long-term support of and association with Holzer's work. As part of the opening of the Guggenheim Museum Bilbao in fall 1997, the artist has been commissioned to create two pieces: a site-specific installation inside a gallery of the Frank Gehry–designed building, and a xenon projection on the Nervión River, which fronts the museum.

This revised edition also marks the last publication written and overseen by Diane Waldman in her capacity as Deputy Director and Senior Curator. It is a fitting reminder of the insight and quality that have been the hallmark of her work at the Guggenheim for more than thirty years.

Thomas Krens, Director
The Solomon R. Guggenheim Foundation

The catalogue that originally accompanied Jenny Holzer's 1989–90 exhibition at the Solomon R. Guggenheim Museum can now be seen as a work in progress. After it sold out, Anthony Calnek, the museum's Director of Publications, and I agreed that a new, updated publication was needed. This revised edition of the catalogue would not have been possible without the support of the artist, whose enthusiasm for the project continued well after the exhibition had concluded.

In the first edition, I wrote, "Jenny Holzer has communicated her messages about modern culture through unbounded outdoor sites and within the controlled interior environments of the gallery and museum." She continues to make use of both indoor and outdoor locations, but recently her work has become more intimate and profound, imbued with a sense of personal loss. As Holzer responds to and reinterprets events in her own life, folding them into the larger issues that confront society, her work continues to find ever-expanding audiences. I am pleased and privileged to be part of that dialogue.

I wish to thank the many individuals who have contributed to this book, in both its original and revised versions. In particular, I would like to single out those whose efforts have made this edition possible. Jerusha Clark, Mary Cross, Brenda Phelps, Jen Rork, Samantha Walsh, Ashley West, and Amy Whitaker at Jenny Holzer's studio provided valuable information and research. At the Guggenheim, thanks are due to Anthony Calnek; Tracey Bashkoff, Curatorial Assistant; Elizabeth Levy, Managing Editor; Jennifer Knox White, Associate Editor; Edward Weisberger, Editor; Carol Fitzgerald, Assistant Editor; Melissa Secondino, Production Assistant; and Keith Mayerson for their skillful contributions in realizing this, the revised and expanded edition.

Diane Waldman

THE LANGUAGE OF SIGNS *Diane Waldman*

Like other artists who first came to prominence in the 1980s, Jenny Holzer is a product of the age of television and the world of advertising. Her work reflects a decade in which originality was suspect. Along with many of her colleagues, she has employed art and aspects of culture to comment on the nature of our age and on the way in which art is perceived and received in a consumer society. As did some of her notable forebears, among them Marcel Duchamp, who used ready-made objects in his work as a way of questioning the traditional role of art in twentieth-century society, and Andy Warhol, who replicated Brillo boxes and other consumer items, Holzer borrows freely from mass culture to explore some of the more pressing issues of our time. Like these earlier artists, she addresses concepts of originality, questioning the value of the artist's hand in the making of a work. But unlike her forerunners, she does so by contrasting the impersonal common object—such as a sign or billboard—with language that is personal and "sincere." In an age of excess, it is increasingly difficult for artists to challenge us, yet Holzer does so. Her texts are often subversive in content, their provocative messages and the mediums in which they are presented testing our assumptions about society and the role of art today.

Holzer's pieces range from simple one-liners to highly complex elegies and meditations on the human condition. Their lean, elegant appearance often masks a complex amalgam of conceptual premise, Pop imagery, and ironic interchange between object and void, presence and absence, sexual desire and individual loss. Holzer communicates her messages in a variety of forms, including printed posters; hand-painted enamel, cast-bronze, and aluminum plaques; granite and marble benches and sarcophaguslike structures; and technological mediums such as electronic signs, television, virtual reality, and the Internet. Her texts have appeared on posters (placed outdoors or in store windows), hats, billboards, benches and sarcophagi, stickers placed on parking meters and inside telephone booths, and in photographs made for magazines. They have been shown in galleries and museums, on the 800-square-foot Spectacolor sign that once commanded Times Square in New York, on the Sony JumboTRON scoreboard in San Francisco's Candlestick Park, on the cable music-video channel MTV, and in other highly visible public places. Her messages, framed in direct, unadorned language, run the gamut of contemporary concerns, among them feminism, gender, AIDS, the environment, class and family structures, war, sexual violence against women, and the nature of power.

Holzer, one of three children, was born in Gallipolis, Ohio, in 1950 and grew up in Lancaster, Ohio. Her mother, who taught riding at a college before her marriage, was an active participant in the community; her father was a car dealer. Holzer drew constantly as a child but stopped when she approached adolescence. She left Lancaster High School after a year to move to Fort Lauderdale, Florida, "to change my life and my lifestyle," she has said.[1] There she attended a private school, Pine Crest Preparatory. She was accepted for early enrollment in the liberal-arts program at Duke University, in Durham, North Carolina, in 1968, but she decided to leave after becoming dissatisfied with the program.

Holzer spent 1970–71 at the University of Chicago, where she took painting, printmaking, and other art courses. Although she liked the curriculum and faculty at Chicago, she left because she was required to take an additional year of liberal-arts courses. Holzer completed her undergraduate work at Ohio University in Athens in 1972, and two years later attended summer school at the Rhode Island School of Design (RISD) in Providence. In 1974, she met fellow RISD student Mike Glier, whom she later married. She began graduate courses in Providence in 1975 and simultaneously worked as a graduate assistant. At this early point in her career, Holzer was an abstract painter, influenced by artists like Mark Rothko and such Color-field painters as Morris Louis. She maintains that she was attracted to the sublime aspect of their art, but feels that her own work was only "pretty good third-generation stripe painting."[2] Among her projects at RISD were a series of paintings in which she incorporated words, a sequence of torn canvases, and a group of pictures based on models of the fourth dimension. For one of her first installation pieces, entitled *The Blue Room*, Holzer painted all the surfaces in her studio—doors, floors, ceilings, windows, and window frames—with a light thalocyanine-blue acrylic wash, creating a disorienting environment in which everything seemed to float. Without intending to, Holzer had created a piece that seemed deliberately to counter the traditions of easel painting, the method promoted by the painting faculty at RISD. The work was deemed so controversial and defiant that it almost led to her expulsion from the school. Holzer tried this new approach to painting, she has commented, because she "really liked the qualities of paint, but I also wanted what you have with a real, not a pictorial space."[3] While still in graduate school, Holzer began to experiment with public art, which she notes was "a kind of precursor to my current work . . . putting things in public and leaving them for people to find, either downtown or at the beach."[4] She explains:

At the beach I would make paintings on long pieces of fabric and leave them so that people would come along and wonder what this thing was that had obviously been left by someone hoping to tickle their imaginations a little bit. Downtown I'd put bread out in abstract patterns so people could watch pigeons eat in squares and triangles. . . . But the works weren't beautiful enough or compelling enough or understandable enough to make people stop.

I had also started a collection of diagrams. . . . I thought that diagrams were the most reduced, the truest way of visual representation. So I collected them . . . and then redrew them . . . And then I put the drawings in a box. I don't know exactly what made me shift, but finally I wound up being more interested in the captions than the drawings. The captions, in a clean, pure way, told you everything. That was the beginning—or one of the beginnings—of what got me to the pure writing.[5]

Holzer turned from a vocabulary of abstract imagery to "pure writing" in 1977, when she began to produce her first series, the *Truisms*. For this series, which occupied her until 1979, her primary medium was language, as it had been for a number of Conceptual artists who directly preceded her. Language fascinated Holzer because she felt that it communicated in a way that painting could not. She had abandoned the idea of writing on her paintings and felt that she was not capable of making narrative or figurative works, yet she wanted to make her feelings about society and culture known.

After being accepted into the Independent Study Program at the Whitney Museum of American Art, Holzer moved to New York in January 1977. The program's reading list, which included studies in art and literature, Marxism, psychology, feminism, social and cultural theory, and criticism, inspired her to create the *Truisms*, which consist of one-liners such as ABUSE OF POWER COMES AS NO SURPRISE, MURDER HAS ITS SEXUAL SIDE, and THE FAMILY IS LIVING ON BORROWED TIME. Her "mock clichés," as she calls them, were her attempt to reformulate important statements by simplifying them. She says, "I started the work as a parody, like the Great Ideas of the Western World in a

nutshell." Her idea was to make "the big issues in culture intelligible as public art."[6] Holzer attempted to represent the great diversity of possible points of view in the *Truisms*, and as a result they often express directly contradictory meanings and feelings. She used the message, the medium, and the public arena to identify and comment upon contradictions and extreme situations in society, communicated in a neutral voice. She attributes the laconic but sincere style of the *Truisms* to her Midwestern background, remarking that "Midwesterners are impatient with things that are either too elaborate or too silly. They want to get things done, so they do it in the most expeditious way—expeditious as in fast and right."[7]

Initially, using a rented typewriter, Holzer typed the *Truisms* on sheets of paper, from which she made printed reproductions. Later, she had the texts set in a sans-serif typeface, Futura Bold Italic (and then in a serif typeface, Times Roman Bold Italic) and printed inexpensively as anonymous posters, which she hung on buildings in SoHo and elsewhere in Manhattan. The posters contained from forty to sixty *Truisms* apiece, arranged alphabetically according to the first word in each sentence. While all the posters were related, each was largely self-contained. The *Truisms* were followed by another poster series, the *Inflammatory Essays*, inspired by Holzer's readings of Emma Goldman, Adolf Hitler, Vladimir Lenin, Mao Tse-tung, and Leon Trotsky, as well as some religious and crackpot writings. Holzer began the series in 1979 and pursued it until 1982. As with all her series, she has since used these writings in a variety of mediums, including electronic signs, benches, and, more recently, Web sites. At first, Holzer deliberately chose to give the *Inflammatory Essays* an informal look by typing them on an old, broken typewriter, but eventually she had them printed on posters in Times Roman Bold Italic. The *Inflammatory Essays* are more structured, political, and exhortatory than the *Truisms*. Moreover, Holzer standardized their format so they could be identified as part of a series: each is a hundred words long and divided into twenty lines, and she had them printed on square sheets of paper of a particular size. While she had presented the *Truisms* in black letters on white paper, Holzer used a different-colored support for each *Inflammatory Essay*, to distinguish one text from another and "to heat up the whole thing."[8]

A resident of lower Manhattan, Holzer came to know and admire a number of the politically oriented artists who worked in the area—

among them John Ahearn, Colen Fitzgibbon, Justin Ladda, Tom Otterness, and Kiki Smith—and worked with them as part of the artists' group Collaborative Projects (Colab). At this time, Holzer considered her work "alternative art." From the posters, Holzer moved on to T-shirts, hats, billboards, and collaborative projects, which included small books. As her work evolved, it moved from terse remarks in relatively ephemeral mediums to a more permanent, large-scale, and authoritative art, from what she called "lower anonymous" to "upper anonymous." In 1980, she began the *Living* series, which consisted of hand-painted enamel and cast-bronze wall plaques with short texts drawn from news items or inspired by mundane activities. She was thus turning away from "Great Ideas" toward an involvement with everyday life.

Holzer's real breakthrough, however, came in 1982, when she worked on a project for the Spectacolor sign in Times Square. This was the first time she used an electronic sign to display her texts. The signs have allowed her to reach a larger audience than she previously commanded. By programming them to run at varying speeds and in different typefaces, colors, and patterns, she is able to evoke nuances of meaning from seemingly matter-of-fact statements. Moreover, the signs are eminently suited to the device of repetition, which Holzer often uses with her swift, accessible consumerist language to engage the viewer in meaningful public discourse. She has also combined electronic signs with other mediums in her installations. At the Barbara Gladstone Gallery, New York, in 1986, Holzer showed LED signs with ten benches made of granite—a new medium for the artist—etched with mordant phrases. The combination of benches and electronic signs was discordant, creating an intense and jarring physical presence. She used a similar combination in *Jenny Holzer: "Laments,"* an installation at the Dia Art Foundation (now the Dia Center for the Arts), New York, in 1989–90: in one room, she displayed an imposing group of LED signs, and in another, an equally compelling but vastly different arrangement of sarcophagi made of granite, marble, and onyx.

The *Truisms* and the series that immediately followed were original yet anonymous in tone. In writing them, Holzer strove to keep some distance between herself and her audience, to depersonalize the writing and to enlarge its meaning from the specific to the general. As she remarks about the *Truisms*, "I try to polish them so they sound as if they had been said for a hundred years, but they're mine."[9] Although Holzer did not set out deliberately to make her work provocative, in at least two instances she ran afoul of the power structure. The first incident occurred in 1982, when the artist was invited to show her work at the Marine Midland Bank in New York. The exhibition, which was installed in the lobby of one of their branches, was taken down after a staff member noticed that one of the *Truisms* read IT'S NOT GOOD TO OPERATE ON CREDIT. Similarly, in 1987, in an installation at The Bourse (a restored Victorian space in Philadelphia used for offices and shops on the site of the former stock exchange), texts from the *Truisms* and the *Survival* series created such an uproar that the signs were turned off. Such passages as IT IS FUN TO WALK CARELESSLY IN A DEATH ZONE, PEOPLE ARE NUTS IF THEY THINK THEY ARE IMPORTANT, and WHAT COUNTRY SHOULD YOU ADOPT IF YOU HATE POOR PEOPLE? were largely responsible for the disruption. The site's sponsors only agreed to turn the signs on again when disclaimers were posted on large boards placed in the vicinity of the installation.

Over the course of the last twenty years, the scope of Holzer's writing has come to encompass not only the social and the political, but also a more subjective and introspective language. The political, social, and sexual slogans of the *Truisms* were replaced by the more complex messages of the *Inflammatory Essays* and the *Survival* series. With the *Laments*, Holzer abandoned the role of narrator and objective observer, the role of the Everyman, as she adopted personal voices to reflect private feelings and thoughts. Her advocacy of social and political issues continued, but her writing lost some of its rhetoric and became more individuated and pensive, with a new emphasis on literature and language rather than on strictly political thought.

Between the *Survival* series and *Laments*, Holzer wrote the *Under a Rock* texts, which she considers a transitional stage in the development toward the very personal and reflective expressions of the *Laments*. In *Under a Rock*, a commentator describes horrific events, as they happen, in a relatively objective tone:

CRACK THE PELVIS SO SHE LIES RIGHT. THIS IS A MISTAKE. WHEN SHE DIES YOU CANNOT REPEAT THE ACT. THE BONES WILL NOT GROW TOGETHER AGAIN AND THE PERSONALITY WILL NOT COME BACK. SHE IS GOING TO SINK DEEP INTO THE MOSS TO GET WHITE AND LIGHTER. SHE IS UNRESPONSIVE TO BEGGING AND SELF-ABSORBED.

The *Laments*, on the other hand, are deeply thoughtful musings on cataclysmic events in the subject's past. In this series, Holzer comments on death and indifference to AIDS and its victims. Whereas the language of *Under a Rock* is active, the *Laments* are introspective and contemplative:

> WITH ONLY MY MIND
> TO PROTECT ME
> I GO INTO DAYS.
> WHAT I FEAR IS
> IN A BOX WITH FUR
> TO MUFFLE IT.
> EVERY DAY I DO NOTHING
> BECAUSE I AM
> SCARED BLANK AND LAZY,
> BUT THEN THE MEN COME.
> I PUT MY MOUTH ON THEM.
> I SPIT AND WRITE
> WITH THE WET.
> THE WET SAYS WHAT
> MUST STOP AND
> WHAT SHALL BEGIN.
> I SPIT BECAUSE THE DEATH
> SMELL IS TOO CLOSE TO ME.
> THE STINK MAKES WORDS
> TELL THE TRUTH ABOUT
> WHO KILLS AND
> WHO IS THE VICTIM.
> DEATH IS THE
> MODERN ISSUE.

Holzer first showed works from what would become her *Laments* series at *Documenta 8* in Kassel, Germany, in 1987. In an installation representing, according to the artist, male and female counterparts, she paired a sarcophagus and LED sign bearing texts written in the voice of a woman with a similar configuration evoking the point of view of a man. She elaborated on this theme in her 1989–90 installation at the Dia Art Foundation, which was composed of thirteen sarcophagi and an equal number of signs. The *Laments* series expresses Holzer's social, political, and personal concerns in more elaborate terms than those of her earlier works; her message is more complex, and she speaks of broader, more universal issues. The language retains a formidable clarity and directness but has a texture and nuance, an elegiac quality that was new to Holzer's work at the time.

The installation at Dia was notable for its drama and heightened sense of urgency. Holzer pulled out all the stops to create an assertive, outspoken piece that controlled and dominated the area it occupied. In a darkened gallery, Holzer's flashing LED signs were positioned vertically and timed to go on at the same time and off at different intervals, eventually leaving the room in total darkness. The sarcophagi, which were placed in an adjacent room, were made in various materials, colors, and sizes: Honey onyx, Verde Antique marble, Ankara Red marble, and Nubian Black granite, ranging from infant- to child- to adult-sized. Each carried an inscription that was reiterated in the vertical signs. Dazzling optical effects and a sense of noise and speed emanated from the flashing red, green, and yellow signs, while silence shrouded the room in which the sarcophagi were found. The emotional disruption created by the contrast could not have been more extreme. This disruption arose also from the work's evocation of two vastly different cultures and time frames, one ancient and the other modern. The installation juxtaposed the tarnished lustre of our Times Square culture with the enduring monuments of ancient Greece; it spoke of ancient cultures and modern myths, of precious materials encasing disintegrating flesh, and of our mortality and the absurd, nihilistic enterprise that is our existence. This theme originated with Holzer's earliest works, but she extended it in the Dia installation in terms of form, language, and imagery.

Also in 1989, Holzer completed *Benches*, an installation at Doris C. Freedman Plaza, at the Sixtieth Street entrance to Central Park in Manhattan, one of a number of works Holzer has developed for public sites. Here, she contrasted two groups of four benches each, one group made of Misty Black granite and inscribed with texts from *Under a Rock*, the other made of white Danby Royal marble inscribed with *Truisms*. The texts were incised at a monument-maker's plant, in a distinctive typeface, Government Style, which was developed by the United States War Department in the 1930s and is still used by the Veterans' Administration on headstones and markers. The benches themselves, which mimicked a certain kind of park bench, conformed to a prototype in general use. Like other site-specific works, such as the sandstone benches incised with selections from *Under a Rock* that Holzer completed in the summer of 1987 for *Skulptur Projekte in Münster*, and in marked contrast to the assertive Dia installation, *Benches* did not dominate its space. Mindful of the very different audiences she was addressing—a select art public at Dia, a much broader one for her outdoor benches—Holzer used very different approaches. Thus, *Benches* was quietly authoritative and understated, yet had a compelling power. Drawn to the familiar shape of the benches—which seemed to belong to the site as part of the entrance to Central Park—viewers sat, read the inscriptions, and compared the two groups of benches. They became absorbed in private contemplation of the texts, gradually becoming aware of the differences in tone and content between the *Truisms* and *Under a Rock* series. Slight variations among the elements of the installation also became apparent; for example, the black granite, *Under a Rock* benches were smaller and contained inscriptions only on the tops of their seats, while the white marble, *Truisms* benches also displayed phrases along the seats' edges. Holzer's uncanny understanding of her audience and her ability to communicate to them made the understated *Benches* far more potent than many other, more insistent public works that had previously been installed at the same site.

Holzer's work more than holds its own both in ideal conditions—in environments for which it has specifically been created and when seen alone—and in more uncontrolled settings, like group exhibitions. In one such exhibition, *Viewpoints: Postwar Painting and Sculpture from the Guggenheim Museum Collection and Major Loans*, at the Guggenheim in the winter of 1988–89, Holzer's inscribed white Danby Royal marble bench *Untitled with Selections from Truisms (A Relaxed Man Is Not . . .)* (1987) had a commanding presence usually associated with much larger works. While it is difficult to account for the magnetism of this quiet work, one can surmise that by virtue of its form, placement, and inscriptions it draws the viewer in the same way that a painting by Vermeer does, controlling a large surrounding space and compelling one to scrutinize it in detail.

Thus, Holzer's work has evolved from casual throwaway texts to highly engineered commercially manufactured signs, which are sometimes accompanied by benches, sarcophagi, or other architectural elements, such as floors, that she has had inscribed with text. Holzer's

installation pieces seem permanent and totemic, no matter how swiftly her messages flash on and off the signs. The message is the medium and then some, and as Holzer has moved from the aphorisms and clichéd ideological phrases of her earlier efforts to deeper meditations on modern life, the human condition, the ravages of AIDS, and violence—from the pronouncements of political figures to an engagement with such literary giants as Samuel Beckett—she has found forms that further enhance her writings. Like the models for the messages in the signs, the prototypes for the benches and sarcophagi also exist in our culture. Unlike the signs, however, the benches and sarcophagi originate not in the vernacular of pop culture, but from other, older traditions. In highlighting many of society's most deeply rooted prejudices, Holzer adds her voice to those of other contemporary artists who have used their art to urge meaningful political reform. That she does so by replicating benches and sarcophagi and by co-opting one of the most blatant forms of commerce—electronic signs used primarily to hype products—reflects her awareness of the power of stereotypes and her ability to appropriate them for her art. In this respect, her work differs significantly from that of Joseph Beuys, an artist to whom she has been compared. Like Beuys, Holzer invests her work with a meaningful political and social agenda; yet Beuys was a German Romantic, a mystic and shaman whose work is founded on the ephemeral, while Holzer is the quintessential American pragmatist, a realist who shares with Pop artists like Warhol the ability to usurp the mass media and use it to make a concrete statement about our culture.

Because much of her work is presented in public surroundings, Holzer is one of the most visible artists on the contemporary scene. Framed in accessible language, her work seeks public response. Location is part of its content, as it is in the work of her predecessors, the Minimalists. Unlike much Minimalist sculpture of the 1960s, however, Holzer's art is both site-specific and self-sufficient, part of a public arena and an entity unto itself. Therefore, the viewer can experience Holzer's work as a member of a group, on a public level, or can interact with it in a more private, intimate way. The Minimalists' approach was based on a rejection of many of the traditional aspects of sculpture and painting. Among their common objectives were the radical simplification of form, the rejection of composition, and the use of industrial materials. Many Minimalists admired abstract artists like Ad Reinhardt, not for the metaphysical content of their work but for their strictly reduced forms. The Minimalists underscored the interaction between work and site, carefully placing their forms within specific environments. This interaction was often interrupted when a piece was removed from its original location; sometimes the work survived in another context, but often the significance of the work was diminished. The Minimalists' neutral geometric shapes, repetitive modular forms, monochromy, and uninflected surfaces are frequently difficult for viewers to comprehend. Because Holzer often adopts vehicles that are a familiar part of our culture, like T-shirts, hats, and electronic signs, her messages are more easily understood. Her use of language is a means of engaging an audience through a shared tool; by contrast, the Minimalists' monochrome canvases, fluorescent tubes, and plywood boxes are often enigmatic to many spectators. Moreover, Holzer's work is more theatrical, seductive, and open to emotion than that of the Minimalists, and the issues she confronts have a broader base. For these reasons, Holzer has reached a segment of the public that often eluded the Minimalists.

While a student at RISD, Holzer was influenced by the magazine *The Fox*, whose editorial board included one of the founders of the Conceptual art movement of the 1960s, Joseph Kosuth. It is important to point out, however, that Holzer's work contrasts markedly with that of Kosuth. Kosuth's conceptual framework is based on texts that already exist, which he isolates and magnifies. His art consists of the act of intervention exercised in the selection of this pre-existing material and is, as Holzer notes, "language on language."[10] Holzer's art is of another order, because she makes statements that sound familiar yet are newly invented and tailored to the specific formats in which they appear. As we have seen, as the meaning of Holzer's work has grown more complex, her forms have changed correspondingly, and her work has taken on a more personal dimension as well as a lyrical and ultimately epic tone. In these respects, her art diverges dramatically from that of the Conceptual artists, which was characterized succinctly by Sol LeWitt:

In conceptual art the idea or the concept is the most important aspect of the work. When an artist uses a conceptual form of art, it means that all of the planning and the decisions are made beforehand and the execution is a perfunctory affair. The idea becomes a machine that makes the art. This kind of art is not theoretical or illustrative of theories; it is intuitive, it is involved with all types of mental processes and it is purposeless. It is usually free from the dependence on the skill of the artist as a craftsman.[11]

In theory, Holzer proceeds from a conceptual frame of reference, mapping out her pieces and having them executed in the manner that LeWitt describes, but in practice, her work does not conform strictly to this model. It does, however, bear close affinities to that of Bruce Nauman. Nauman synthesizes Minimalist and Conceptualist attitudes but infuses his art with a distinctive individualism that sets it apart from either aesthetic. Holzer shares with Nauman these characteristics as well as a laconic style, a black sense of humor, an acute awareness of the absurd, and a willingness to tackle such compelling subjects as sex, violence, and death. Both take advantage of ready-made forms and language, but where Nauman portrays himself in his work, Holzer focuses chiefly on language as image rather than on imagery per se. And whereas Nauman's work remains more clearly within the Minimalist and Conceptualist canons he was instrumental in defining, Holzer, a younger artist, has formed her own critical vocabulary of language and signs and uses a public rather than private forum as a means to convey her concerns.

In working with language, Holzer is heir to a twentieth-century artistic tradition that began with Cubist painting and collage and has figured prominently in many of the major movements of our time, including Futurism, Dada, Surrealism, Abstract Expressionism, and Pop and Conceptual art. Written language has been used to refer to the real world, exploited for its potential as pure form, juxtaposed with images, and employed to replace images altogether. In her 1989–90 installation at Dia, Holzer brought a new resonance to this tradition. The heroic and noble Dia installation embodied qualities of the more ambitious American painting of the 1950s, even as it retained some of the worldliness of Pop art together with aspects of Minimalism and Conceptual art. The chapel-like mood and attendant religious aura that the Dia installation evoked bring to mind the paintings of Rothko. While Holzer does not emulate the colors or forms of Rothko's work, her signs emit an enveloping, atmospheric color, and she has developed her own basic language that, in its emotive power and simplicity, recalls that of Rothko. Although her work embraces irony and humor, she, like Rothko—and like Barnett

Newman, whose art hers also resembles in its formal clarity, scale, and grandeur—touches upon the metaphysical dimensions of life. In the Dia installation, her language extended beyond the tangible, the here and now, and reached into the abyss.

Equally ambitious but entirely different in scope was Holzer's installation for the Solomon R. Guggenheim Museum, also in 1989–90. The installation was composed of three distinct parts: an LED sign, over 530 feet long, which ran along the exterior of the parapet wall that encloses the museum's ramps; a set of benches in the High Gallery; and another set of benches on the ground floor of the rotunda. The flamboyant spiraling tricolor LED sign displayed a selection of all of Holzer's writings to date—*Truisms*, *Inflammatory Essays*, texts from the *Living* and *Survival* series, *Under a Rock*, and *Laments*—as well as the first version of a new work, *Mother and Child*, an intimate statement about the nature of motherhood and the artist's feelings for her daughter, Lili, born in May 1988. (Holzer expanded on this theme in her installation for the 1990 Venice *Biennale*.) The twenty-seven austere Bethel White granite benches in the High Gallery featured selections from the *Living* series. The seventeen warm-toned Indian Red granite benches on the rotunda floor, dramatically placed in a circle, contained selections from the *Survival* series.

From the beginning stages of the project, Holzer had determined that she wanted to work with the spaces of the Frank Lloyd Wright building to make a site-specific installation that would create a dialogue with Wright's edifice. Initially, she conceived of the LED sign being accompanied by a series of benches installed in alcoves behind the museum's main elevator. She had not planned on using either the High Gallery or the rotunda floor, but after numerous visits to the museum over a period of more than a year, she became convinced of the need to anchor the sign with installations in those spaces. The artist then commissioned Rutland Marble and Granite, located in Vermont, to fabricate and incise the benches to her specifications. She also worked with Sunrise Systems, a Boston-area firm, who built the customized sign. Once the sign was placed in position in the museum's rotunda, she was able to fine-tune the program of her texts on site. As the longest and most technologically advanced sign she had used to date, it provided her with the opportunity to employ many new patterns and speeds.

None of Holzer's planning predicted the end result. The installation dramatically transformed the Wright-designed space. The LED sign underscored the active nature of the rotunda's spiral shape, an organic form used by Wright to convey his belief in nature's power. Holzer contrasted this with the quiet, enclosed space of the High Gallery, while merging the active and the passive in the arrangement of curved benches on the rotunda floor. As she had at Dia, Holzer took a series of spaces and enlivened them with a few understated but potent forms and an equally basic but dazzling array of colors. Holzer's installation was positively theatrical. It captured the force and energy of Wright's design without yielding any of Holzer's own form and rhetoric.

While the Guggenheim installation shared aspects of Holzer's work at Dia, it also differed substantially from the earlier piece. The enclosed galleries at Dia were suited to a chapel-like effect, but the Guggenheim's building is a more open, public form of architecture. In this context, some of Holzer's most private statements—as well as the provocative, combative texts—became part of a larger, public discourse. The many profiles reflected in Holzer's writing—lover, mother, feminist, psycho, populist—were revealed to an audience largely unaccustomed to her work.

Viewers were mesmerized by the installation. Holzer utilized the power of the media to command, control, and manipulate, combining a popular idiom—the LED sign—with 1980s activism and issue-oriented writing to urge her audience to confront topics of overriding concern. The sign was programmed in a sequence of twenty-one cycles, the 330 messages linked by a basic pattern with a few variations. The entire program was one hour and forty-five minutes in length, at the end of which it was repeated from the beginning. The audience could view the entire program or only a portion. Many elected to see the complete version and some stayed to watch the cycle repeat itself. Holzer's language was powerful, evocative, and forthright, its pain and longing undeniable. The program had a hypnotic effect on many spectators, as the artist's customary complement of colors—red, yellow, and green—and the way in which passages overlapped one another or terminated before another began created a visually dazzling panorama; words often blurred into illegible forms as they spun around the ramp at great speed.

Holzer's ability to accommodate spectacle in her work was nowhere more evident than in the Guggenheim installation. As provocative, though far less assertive, than the LED sign were the benches in the

High Gallery and on the rotunda floor, Their stone surfaces were incised with texts such as YOU ARE CAUGHT THINKING ABOUT KILLING ANYONE YOU WANT. The groupings of benches created quiet oases where one could sit and ponder the exhibition. But it was the spiraling sign—following the course of the rising ramps and enhancing the futuristic nature of Wright's visionary architecture—that gave added urgency to the public dimension of Holzer's discourse. Though her work was silent, the drama she created with her words and lights made the building resound, conjuring the ideals of the great architect himself. The work of the artist and the architect—both moralists and both artists—lent credence to each other; this special collaboration revealed each in a new light.

For her installation in the United States Pavilion at the 1990 Venice *Biennale*, Holzer made a number of advance visits to the city and found she was intrigued with its feeling. In particular, she was fascinated by spaces like the waiting room at the Doge's Palace, where Venetian citizens waiting for an audience had worn away portions of the marble floor. Holzer knew early on that she wanted to create a work, using Venetian materials, that would make reference to Venetian customs. To this end, she covered the floors of the pavilion's two antechambers with marble that had been finished at an Italian stone yard. Tiles of white Biancone, red Magnaboschi, and black Marquina marble were placed in a diamond pattern—in red and black in one room and red and white in the other, a color scheme reminiscent of the Doge's Palace. Selections from *Truisms* in five different languages were incised into the red tiles. Benches lined the perimeter of each antechamber: in one, the bench tops were made of white marble and inscribed with selections from *Mother and Child* (the text that premiered at the Guggenheim), and in the other, they were made of red marble and inscribed with writing from the *Inflammatory Essays*. Holzer's installation also occupied two galleries in the pavilion. In one, Holzer covered the floor in red marble and installed twenty-one horizontal LED signs on three of the walls, on which writing from all of her series to date (in English, French, German, Italian, and Spanish) were shown. The other gallery, the most effective room of the installation, had a red, black, and white marble floor with twelve vertical LED signs that displayed the *Mother and Child* text. As the marble floor reflected the light emitted from the signs, the borders between sign and floor blurred, creating a space that seemed to be of another time and

another dimension. Caught up in this disembodied space, one felt that one was in the Doge's antechamber, a spirit among the many others, part of the time and timelessness that is so much a part of Venice.

Together with her installation at the United States Pavilion, Holzer's writings were placed on an LED sign above a luggage carousel at Marco Polo airport (with texts in German, English, and Italian), at Santa Lucia train station, and in the backseats of taxis in the outer suburb of Mestre. Placards were featured on the vaporetti that travel along the city's canals. Hats and T-shirts containing her messages were sold at souvenir stands along the Zattere (the promenade that overlooks the Giudecca Canal) and in the area around the Rialto bridge. In addition, broadcasts of her texts, each ten to fifteen seconds long, appeared at random intervals on Italian television.

Following its presentation at the United States Pavilion, *The Venice Installation* traveled to several locations in Europe and the United States. In 1992, while she was working on the installation, Holzer began a new series of texts, collectively entitled *War*. The series was formed in response to the events of the Gulf War, which was being covered extensively by the cable-television channel CNN. The texts included the following:

BURNED ALL OVER SO ONLY HIS TEETH ARE GOOD, HE SITS FUSED TO THE TANK. METAL HOLDS THE BLAST HEAT AND THE SUN. HIS DEATH IS FRESH AND THE SMELL PLEASANT. HE MUST BE PULLED AWAY SKIN SPLITTING. HE IS A SUGGESTION THAT AFFECTS PEOPLE DIFFERENTLY.

The series of fourteen texts was first shown in June 1992, on vertical LED signs in the stairwell of the Kunsthalle Basel as part of a group exhibition entitled *Transform*. In the fall of 1993, the texts were displayed at the church of St. Peter in Cologne. The church formed an appropriate setting for the writings as it had been bombed during World War II. Holzer placed LED signs along the columns of the church's rebuilt interior and between the stained-glass windows that had replaced the original fenestration destroyed by the bombing.

Holzer stopped writing the *War* texts because she felt they were "too over the top,"[12] but she returned to the theme of war in 1993, in a series entitled *Lustmord* (a German phrase best translated as "sex murder") spurred by the tragic events in war-torn Bosnia. These texts, which focus on violence perpetrated against women, are, Holzer says, "sadder, scarier, yet more restrained than *War.*" Based on a range of sources, including news items citing atrocities committed by Serbian soldiers against Muslim women, the texts were written from three points of view: the victim, the perpetrator, and an observer. In contrast to Holzer's earlier *Laments*, the series of writings focusing on death and mourning in which the voices speak from their graves, in the *Lustmord* series, as Holzer has noted, the victim is alive when she speaks. Holzer has said that it was "easier [for her] to write in the guise of the perpetrator than as the victim," perhaps because it was more difficult for her to convey her anguish as the victim than to express her fury in the role of the perpetrator. The observer texts are mournful in tone, reflecting Holzer's own recent personal losses: the deaths of her mother, with whom she was particularly close, and that of her father within a year of each other. The voices in *Lustmord* range in emotion from sadness, frustration, pity, and disgust in face of the violations and suffering witnessed by the observer, to savagery and despair. Chillingly, the series underscores the way the world often sits by, watching, while women fall prey to abuse and death.

The *Lustmord* texts first appeared in November 1993 in the German publication *Süddeutsche Zeitung Magazin*.[13] Inside were thirty photographs of the texts written in ink, in both German and English, on various parts of women's bodies, including I AM AWAKE IN THE PLACE WHERE WOMEN DIE and THE COLOR OF HER WHERE SHE IS INSIDE OUT IS ENOUGH TO MAKE ME KILL HER. On the cover of the magazine was a card on which two texts were printed, one in ink made from blood donated by women from Germany and the former Yugoslavia. The cover created a furor and was widely debated in the press, because it appeared at the same time that some blood supplies in Germany were found to contain the HIV virus, despite official reports that they had tested negative.

"In war," Holzer stated in an interview that accompanied the photographs of her texts, "rape is normal. . . . It is part of [the soldier's] income, so to speak, a payment in kind." Holzer agreed that the language she used is "pornographic and precise." She wanted to use graphic language to make the violence, anger, and despair forcibly vivid, so that the texts would convey the experiences of suffering and death. She stated that "realistic representation runs the risk of being misused as pornography again. The most perverse example is the documentary material about crimes in Yugoslavia that is being sold as pornographic videos—and they are bringing the highest price."[14] The language of the *Lustmord* texts is similar in some ways to that of the *Truisms*, though the voices of the *Truisms* are those of Midwesterners, like the artist herself; Holzer also used multiple voices, as she did in the *Truisms*, to identify distinct points of view. The subject of *Lustmord*—sexual violence against women—reflects cataclysmic events, as had earlier series, such as *Under a Rock* and *Laments*.

Holzer presented the second manifestation of the *Lustmord* texts in an installation at the Barbara Gladstone Gallery, New York, in May–June 1994. Within the darkened recesses of the gallery, Holzer placed a hut, a vaulted structure composed of metal and wood with a doorway at one end. The red leather that covered the hut's interior was embossed with patterns and Holzer's texts. In the floor, she used a lattice-and-floral design. On the walls, the *Lustmord* texts were arranged within a diamond-shaped pattern that conveyed the look of a chain-link fence, with a letter placed in the middle of each diamond. The texts were separated into three parts: the victim's words to the left as one entered the hut, the perpetrator's at the center, and the observer's at the right. The stock lettering and regularized format, and the deafening silence that surrounded the viewer, created a sense of foreboding in the darkened chamber, bringing to mind the inhumanity of a concentration camp. A cylindrical LED sign, which showed her texts in 3-D, was positioned in the center of the hut, and another stood outside its entrance. This was the first time Holzer used this type of sign; in them, the texts seem to float and collide, appear and disappear in a transparent shell. On a table in another section of the gallery, Holzer displayed human bones, some of which were encircled, like relics of human suffering tagged as fragments of war, with small silver bands engraved or etched with text. As in Holzer's benches, meaning was conveyed by both perceptual and tactile means, for Holzer intended viewers to handle the bones and read their inscriptions. They recalled "reliquaries," "women's secrets," and "mass death," according to the artist, and the silver served as a "crude allusion to the fact that these deaths, any death has value."

For this installation, Holzer was faced with the issue of how to represent the hideous nature of atrocities perpetrated against women. While she could have relied on an earlier format to memorialize the victims of this violence, such as the granite and marble sarcophagi, she instead chose to create a stark but striking juxtaposition of the primitive and the technological, in the contrast betweeen the hut and the LED signs. While the hut recalls nomadic modes of existence, it also embodies references to the womb; here, it is scored by writing, as if in some ritual mutilation. The embossed texts also evoke the names of the dead and missing-in-action that are inscribed on war memorials.

The sophisticated hardware and provocative imagery of this piece did not serve an illustrative function, but rather were used to invoke disembodied voices of abuse and power. Holzer's cool method of presentation reflects the news media's presentation of such horrific events to the public, paralleling the secondhand way in which audiences, as passive spectators, experience the most shocking brutalities. In contrast to this ritualized anonymity, the display of bones personalized the sense of atrocity, for their silver tags were made, in an act of grief and loss, from the melted-down remains of some of Holzer's mother's belongings. *Lustmord*, then, is both a statement of collective suffering and a private message of individual pain.

In 1996, at the invitation of Klaus Werner and the Förderkreis der Leipziger Galerie für Zeitgenössische Kunst, Holzer created an installation at the Völkerschlachtdenkmal in Leipzig. The Völkerschlachtdenkmal was commissioned by the German Patriotic League in 1913 as a memorial to the 1813 Battle of Nations. The structure itself—a truncated pyramid, over 300 feet tall and adorned with colossal statues of men in armor—was intended to symbolize such wartime values as national power, courage, perseverance, and military triumph. Since 1913, the monument and its values have appealed to political parties as disparate as monarchists, Nazis, and communists. For *KriegsZustand*, meaning "state of war," Holzer used laser beams to project German translations of texts from *Lustmord* and other series onto the monument and its reflecting pool. Through her texts, she addressed subjects that are as much aspects of wartime as the values celebrated by the Völkerschlachtdenkmal, though they are taboo: fear, abuse of power, rape, torture, loss of human dignity, and terror.

Holzer has been involved with several other outdoor projects in Europe since the early 1990s, among them *BLACK GARDEN*, in the town of Nordhorn, Germany, and *Erlauf Monument*, in Erlauf, Austria. *BLACK GARDEN* is one of a number of "antiheroic" memorials that have been erected throughout Germany in the last few years. Holzer was asked by town officials and a citizens' group (after a member had seen

her work in the 1987 *Skulptur Projekte in Münster*) to prepare a proposal for Langemarckplatz, the site of a memorial to Germany's fallen soldiers. The square had once featured a bronze statue of a naked youth, but after being removed by the SS in 1933, it was later replaced with a metal dish that held an eternal flame, which sat on the original circular sandstone plinth. The plinth bears the inscription, "The living stand upon those who have fallen." On a nearby brick wall are twenty-three bronze plaques, installed in the 1950s, commemorating the dead of World War II. One of these is dedicated to the victims of political and racial persecution from 1933 to 1945.

Holzer stripped the site of the existing grass, flowers, and foliage, replacing them with Black Mondo grass, a black apple tree, and other plants to create an ebony-colored garden. The only exception to the predominantly black planting is a group of white flowers under the plaque honoring political and racial victims. Holzer also added five benches made of local red sandstone to the site. These were inscribed with texts, in both German and English, from her series *War*:

IT IS THE WAR ZOO. IT IS A LANDMARK. PILOTS NAME IT. THE ANIMAL IS FOLDED IN THE LANDSCAPE. A BONE IS BROKEN SO IT CANNOT MOVE AWAY. INSTINCT MAKES IT WATCHFUL. IT EXPECTS THAT SOMEONE WILL TOUCH IT TO RESTORE THE PACT.

Holzer's plans included the removal of the original memorial. Amid considerable controversy, however, and only after the garden had been inaugurated, on October 28, 1994, Holzer suceeded in having the eternal flame removed, but not the plinth on which it sat.

For *BLACK GARDEN* to survive, it has to be tended by the community, a reparative act that acknowledges the German people's collective grief, loss, shame, and anger in connection with the two world wars. The garden is a reminder that individuals share a common memory, and suggests that only by acknowledging the horrors of war can we strive for peace.

In contrast to the brooding quality of *BLACK GARDEN*, Holzer's *Erlauf Monument* (1995) is a study in light. This project resulted when Franz Kuttner, Mayor of Erlauf, Austria, proposed that two artists—one from the United States and the other from the former Soviet Union—be invited to create artworks commemorating the historic meeting between Major General Stanley E. Reinhart, Commanding General of the 65th U.S. Infantry Division, and Major General D. A. Drickhin, General of the 7th U.S.S.R. Air and Land Division, at midnight on May 8, 1945, in Erlauf, when they shook hands to officially acknowledge the unconditional surrender of Nazi Germany. Holzer and sculptor Oleg Komov were invited to take part. Two traffic islands, located near each other in the center of town, had been selected as the sites for their works. Komov (who died before the dedication of the site) conceived a symbolic representation of Austria, in the form of a sculpture of a tiny girl caught between two giants, depicting the Soviet Union and the United States. Holzer created a very different type of monument. Referring to the bombing raids of World War II, she installed a searchlight, which projects vertically over one mile before dissolving into the sky. The light emanates from an octagonal base made of Bethel White granite, which is surrounded by white plantings, including a circle of birch trees. Pathways of Bethel White granite lead to and from the searchlight, one of the paths joining Holzer's light with Komov's sculpture. A new series of writings, the *Erlauf* texts, were cut into the stones of the paths:

ALWAYS POLITE TO OFFICERS

SMILING OFTEN TO DISARM

THE ENERGETICALLY CRUEL

BLOOD OUTSIDE FOR ANIMALS

A MEMORY OF DOMINANCE

THE SOLDIER BITES YOUR STOMACH

SNEAKING TO WASH

THE HORSE RUNNING INTO WALLS

NEW TEETH IN THE BABY'S MOUTH

THE BABY MOVES TO YOUR OTHER BREAST

ADDING WATER TO FOOD

FULL OF SWALLOWED BLOOD

SON OF A RAPIST

THE CHILD WITH A HAND IN HER

BIRDS EATING THEM

PROPERTIES SEIZED BY THE ZEALOUS

YOUR MOTHER WITH NO REAL POWER

THINKING WHILE HELD DOWN

AGREEING TO STAY STILL

WAITING TO BE TRANSPORTED

Veterans from the United States and the former Soviet Union attended the dedication of the monument in the spring of 1995. Holzer's monument preserves memories of the past without celebrating them, conveying its message through the viewer's act of remembering. Although fifty years have passed since the declaration of peace it commemorates, the monument warns that war is not to be forgotten and that peace can only be maintained through constant vigilance.

1. Interview with the artist by Diane Waldman, June 6 and July 12, 1989. Excerpts from this interview appear on pp. 31–35 of this publication.

2. Quoted in Bruce Ferguson, "Wordsmith: An Interview with Jenny Holzer by Bruce Ferguson," in *Jenny Holzer: Signs*, exh. cat. (Des Moines: Des Moines Art Center, 1986), p. 66.

3. Quoted in Michael Auping, *Jenny Holzer*, Universe Series on Women Artists (New York: Universe, 1992), p. 72.

4. Quoted in Ferguson, p. 66.

5. Quoted in ibid.

6. Quoted in James Danziger, "American Graffiti," *The Sunday Times Magazine* (London), December 4, 1988, p. 5.

7. Quoted in Ferguson, p. 65.

8. Quoted in Diana Nemiroff, "Personae and Politics" (interview), *Vanguard* 12 (November 1983), p. 26.

9. Quoted in Jeanne Siegel, "Jenny Holzer's Language Games" (interview), *Arts Magazine* 60, no. 4 (December 1985), p. 65.

10. Quoted in ibid.

11. Sol LeWitt, "Paragraphs on Conceptual Art," *Artforum* 5, no. 10 (summer 1967), p. 80.

12. This and all following quotations, unless otherwise indicated, are from an interview with the artist by Diane Waldman, March 8, 1994.

13. *Süddeutsche Zeitung Magazin*, November 19, 1993. The magazine, which has a circulation of 400,000, began devoting one issue a year to an artist in 1990. Francisco Clemente, Anselm Kiefer, and Jeff Koons are among the other artists whose work has been featured.

14. Christian Kämmerling, "'Der Tod ist keine hygienische Angelegenheit'" (interview with Holzer), *Süddeutsche Zeitung Magazin*, November 19, 1993, p. 34.

DW: You mentioned to me that at the Rhode Island School of Design you were doing canvases with writing on them. Is that how you began writing? How did you begin doing public projects?

JH: When I started at RISD, I was an abstract painter. But when I was in graduate school there, I became interested in having identifiable subject matter, and I didn't want to paint it. I wanted to get content in there, something different from the content of abstract art. I eventually tried writing bits of found information on the canvases. And at the same time, I began working on public projects. I left pieces of my paintings around for people to come across. These were for the most part unsatisfactory experiments because what I left was basically meaningless to the people who found it. The one encouraging thing was that I knew it was theoretically possible to leave things for people that would stop them in their tracks. If I could ever figure out what was going to be of interest to them, people were willing and able to study or enjoy or worry or fight over what I left there.

DW: Was there an intent on your part to reach a mass audience, as against, say, a RISD audience?

JH: I wanted to see if I could make anything that would be of use to or have some kind of meaning for a general audience, people on their way to lunch who didn't care anything about art. I didn't manage that at RISD, but that was what I tried to do, and I suppose this went hand-in-hand with needing to come up with the proper subject matter. If you want to reach a general audience, it's not art issues that are going to compel them to stop on the way to lunch, it has to be life issues.

DW: Did these ideas take more concrete shape as a result of your enrollment in the Whitney program, or just from your move to New York?

JH: Both. My thinking became sharper from the shock of moving to New York, where it was clear that if you were going to present something to people, it better be just right, it better be something genuinely interesting because otherwise people weren't going to give it a second glance. It was a combination of getting a feel for the environment in New York and receiving help from the staff at the

Whitney, who gave me a wonderful, far-flung reading list—great books of Western knowledge. This confirmed my suspicion that the world is the subject for art, or at least for my art.

DW: What in particular triggers your writing?

JH: A combination of reading and events in the world and whatever is going on with my life.

DW: What kind of writing interests you? I think your writing has a directness that is in some ways specifically American.

JH: I have always admired two kinds of writing. One, delirious, flaming, emotional writing and two, pure, pared-down, essential writing. I also like writing that has gears, that is a certain way and then shifts.

DW: The two polarities you are talking about, in a way you are doing that with your work, in terms not only of the writing but also of the outdoor context and indoor context, the changes in size—small pieces, large pieces—public pieces, private pieces, randomness and control. Can we discuss the elements of randomness and control in your work?

JH: I try not to make it completely random or sloppy, but there has to be a wild part. In the writing, you have to go off into the stratosphere and then come back down. That's what I like, when things spin out of control but then are pulled back so that they're yours. I want them to be accessible, but not so easy that you throw them away after a second or two.

DW: I think you are capturing what both life and art are about— randomness, order, being out of control, being in control . . . both life and art have these dimensions.

JH: I don't want total control and I don't want complete chaos. But both there in their extreme forms, not averaged.

DW: Was it after you started the Whitney program that you began doing the posters?

JH: I started writing the *Truisms* when I was at the Whitney, and I was in the program when I printed the first poster.

DW: After you did the *Truisms*, how did you develop the concept for the *Inflammatory Essays*?

JH: I remember that I thought the tone of the *Truisms* was possibly too even, too bland, too balanced. I wanted less balance, and I wanted the next writing to flame. I tried to figure out what form would be uneasy and hot, and I went to the manifesto. I'm being kind of flip saying unbalanced and flaming—I also wanted a passionate statement about the way the world could be if people did things right. I wanted to move between, or include both sorts of manifesto making, one being scary, an inflamed rant to no good end, and then the positive type, a deeply felt description of how the world should be. I went to the library to find examples of lunatic manifestos and beautiful ones.

DW: Did you feel that the subject matter of the *Inflammatory Essays* lent itself to a larger number of words than in the *Truisms*?

JH: Sure, it's hard to rant in one sentence. I needed to have at least a paragraph. Also, at that stage, I was a little bored with writing one-liners, and I thought it would be interesting to expand. So I went to my natural limit of one paragraph.

DW: Why did you begin to use the electronic signs?

JH: I started using them because I thought the posters had underground or alternative connotations, and I felt that the signs were the official voice of everything from advertising to public-service announcements. Plus they're of the world. Also, on the most basic level, it's a good format for displaying writing. That's why they're used for news blurbs, for short bursts of information. Plus I'm attracted to the way they look. They're modern and they appeal to me the same way they do to a lot of people. They flash and have nice colors and all that stuff.

DW: It's difficult now to disassociate any electronic sign from yours. So

I have a hard time when I walk around New York, trying to figure out whether you've written certain signs or not. It reverses the way you think about something that is in the real world. I would assume that you like this aspect of it?

JH: I enjoy that kind of confusion. I am happy when my material is mixed with advertisements or pronouncements of some sort or another. That lends a certain weight to my things, makes them part of real life. It also creates some very funny juxtapositions.

DW: Were the works in the *Living* series done as aluminum or bronze plaques and then as electronic signs?

JH: Actually, the very first ones I did were hand-lettered metal signs, the kind sign painters make that say, "This Way to Fire Escape." Typically, they have red or black letters on a white enamel surface. Soon after, I made the cast-bronze plaques, and finally the writing appeared on electronic signs.

DW: At this time were you reading anything different from what we talked about in terms of the earlier series?

JH: I didn't go to the library for the *Living* series because I wanted to change my way of working and the tone of the writing. For the *Living* series, I went to a moderate voice and temperate language because I thought this would match the subject: everyday events that just happened to have some kink in them. The writing described these events and then offered an absurdity or some sociopolitical observation.

DW: Was the *Survival* series done only on the LED and UNEX signs?

JH: The *Survival* series was mostly done for the electronic signs but I also made aluminum plaques. Since the language was flat, dull aluminum seemed like the right kind of material.

DW: You primarily used bronze in the *Living* series—why do you distinguish between aluminum and bronze? Is it only because aluminum has that flatness?

JH: I did this to separate the series from each other and to make it easier to recognize each one. That's why I changed from bronze plaques in the *Living* series, which have a traditional serif typeface, to the aluminum plaques, which have a contemporary sans-serif face. The contemporary face matched aluminum, a modern material. Plus the subject of survival seemed to be a modern preoccupation.

DW: What does the title *Under a Rock* connote?

JH: It refers to my bringing up unmentionable or at least unpleasant topics—things that crawl out from under rocks. It is something like what I did in the *Inflammatory Essays*.

DW: Can you tell us about any literary influences or any reading that you did in particular for *Under a Rock*?

JH: There was nothing specific for this series. In a way, for *Under a Rock*, I was able to combine elements of the *Living* series and the *Survival* series with the *Inflammatory Essays*. I wanted the language to be hotter and more peculiar than the deadpan delivery of the *Living* series and the *Survival* series, but I didn't want the ideological ranting of the *Inflammatory Essays*. I decided to write about the real consequences of politics. Hence, people throwing bodies in the river, mothers running from war and terror—man-made catastrophe. What actually happens to people as a result of unnecessary disaster is the theme of *Under a Rock*. It's what occurs after people have overcome or have been overcome.

DW: Samuel Beckett as well as Edgar Lee Masters's *Spoon River Anthology* are often mentioned as possible inspirations for the *Laments*. I don't want necessarily to imply a direct link with these sources, but I wonder if you will clarify any connection that may exist.

JH: I had started the *Laments* and had done maybe half a dozen of them when my husband, Mike, brought *Spoon River Anthology* to me. I don't think it was a direct influence, but it was nice to see how somebody else made dead people talk. It was interesting because Masters let many people speak, horrible people and wonderful people. Then Beckett is simply an all-purpose hero for me.

DW: I think that your own predilections are not unlike Beckett's, that what you're trying to say is succinct, it's black humor, it's ironic.

JH: But deadly serious.

DW: I would like to ask you about your changing during the last few years from the use of posters or electronic signs alone to signs used together with benches or sarcophagi. It seems to me to put you into another sphere.

JH: Even when I was concentrating on public projects, I was exhibiting some residue or artifacts from these public events in art spaces. I gradually came to think that since I was showing pieces as art, it would make sense to design some things specifically for indoor spaces. As I became more confident that I could keep the public stuff going, and sure of my abiding interest in it, I felt I could do the art stuff and not kill the public work. I wanted to be completely satisfied with what I put indoors, and to do that, I had to think the same way that I did in the outdoor projects, which was to design things especially for the situation.

DW: I find that there's a certain power to those "official" art efforts that you don't quite get in an outdoor context. If you are in an outdoor context, you have a sign that moves, that changes quickly, and you also have a transient group of people. In an indoor context, you have a fixed space and a body of work that was done for a particular purpose. I think there is a tendency to stay longer. I don't know if this is because of a change you have consciously made in the work or if it results from the setting.

JH: What I gain outdoors is the surprise that a passerby has from seeing something unexpected, something with hard content. That's lost indoors. It's almost impossible to shock an art audience. With the outdoor work you might startle people so much that you have a prayer of changing their thinking a little bit, or even prompting them to take some kind of action. You have an incrementally better chance of altering something in the world with the public work because you reach more people. And because the content of the writing is taken at face value, it is not dismissed as art.

However, what you gain indoors is the chance to develop a complex presentation of a lot of ideas. The installation that you set up can be more intricate, the writing can be more complicated, the ideas can be elaborated, the emotional tone can be richer—you have more layers. The "art" might be better. I'm not even sure I mean that—often I think a stripped-down public thing is just as fine. I'm not sure that I have a preference. I like to do both.

DW: It is also conceivable to me that you can take some of the content of an indoor piece and make it work in the outdoors.

JH: Oh yes! They're not mutually exclusive, although they're starting to be more separate than they were. It used to be that the exact same stuff would live in both places.

DW: In the work with the sarcophagi you're using an idiom that is difficult, because of its meanings, for even the most knowledgeable person to take into his or her home.

JH: I hope the sarcophagi are difficult and shocking. When you're working in an art space it's hard to create the reaction that you get when you encounter things on the street, so a "difficult" form is useful. Death is a hard subject.

DW: The benches and sarcophagi have a lot of power. Do you find that certain forms are more effective than others, regardless of size?

JH: Sometimes I use neutral forms, and other times I want loaded objects like sarcophagi. It has to do with trying to find and convey meaning. If you can choose the subject and then find an appropriate, functional form, you are home free. I try to get the content and present it in the correct way and on the right thing; I find a home for it, and then I put it where someone is going to see it. Even the street posters, even the *Inflammatory Essays*, I wanted to be nice in their own horrible way. They had to have form. It was important that they were purposeful. For example, I wanted the typeface for the *Essays* to be italic and bold and just so. The posters had to be brightly colored and to be pure squares so that people would want to come up to them. It's just taking care.

DW: And it's seduction.

JH: And seduction. Careful seduction.

DW: Do you get any special reactions to your work from women?

JH: I've noticed some particular responses from women. Women are very concerned about the nuts and bolts of survival. Women often feel more threatened; they are a little more aware than men, a little sadder about realities or possible consequences. Maybe that's a reason why some of my subjects resonate with women. Another reason is that women are very practical because they have to be, and my approach can be practical and explicit.

DW: I think that the work has a directness and clarity to it, whether it's the shape or the writing.

JH: Both, hopefully. I think women appreciate the functional.

DW: Should we talk about the piece you are doing for the Guggenheim? Can you tell us what you have seen in the space, which is very organic in nature, and how you envision it will be in contrast to the space at Dia, which was fairly regular and much more enclosed? Do you see the museum's shape as leading you to something different from the way you are working?

JH: It's an intriguing proposition at the museum. This is a place where you can't ignore the shape or the volume of the space. I thought for a long time that it would be incredible to do something with the building, not against it, not for it, just with it. So I tried to come up with a piece that would be integrated, but that would add something. It has to be somewhere between autonomous and respectful. I think going around and around the parapet wall with a sign will do that— the work will have a life of its own but certainly will give more than a nod to the space. I hope the piece won't be overcome by the architecture or ruin it. I think it will be a logical shape within the space. People will be able to get information from the spiral sign while standing below, on the rotunda floor, or standing across the space on a ramp. The sign should pass the visibility test, and with good programming, it should be appealing. The work must be engaging somehow, physically and emotionally. It should look relatively clean. It shouldn't be excessive.

DW: This is fascinating because the central space is so much a part of the volume of the place, yet it hasn't been used before. Even sculptors who have looked at the space and made pieces specifically for it have really used only the rotunda floor. They haven't considered the parapet, which ties the whole place together from the dome to the main floor.

JH: The ramp with its parapet wall is where you get up and down, where you travel. It's a nice band, a nice ribbon. It is such a strong visual element, so it seemed the place to go. What I would like to do, if the sign guys and I can manage it, is to have periods of calm in the sign's programming, texts spiraling slowly. That will be the dominant mode because it will be like water flowing, going round and round. But then I would like to break the pattern and have texts go to the center, flash and twist, be still, and then continue.

DW: The piece at Dia has some of that.

JH: Yes, it's funny, it's only after you stare at a space a long time that you figure out what it requires. For Dia, I'd done all the programming in advance, and each sign was to act independently of the other. I'd done all-out special effects, with every sign going crazy. Then when I got to the installation, I realized that because of the subject matter, the setting should be very quiet. It was best if there was, for the most part, a steady, slow-rising, synchronized text on each sign. They should play one by one, stop when they finish their program, and then go black. And after the last sign stopped, they should all light again simultaneously so there would be a little glory and optimism. But this came clear to me only three days before the show opened. I imagine that I'll do last-minute changes at the Guggenheim too.

DW: Will there be a particular theme for the writing in the Guggenheim piece? Will it be a statement about yourself, about museums, about art? Will it reflect a particular response to the setting in comparison to your response to Dia?

JH: The expanse of parapet wall gives me a long billboard on which I can display a lot of material. I'll go back into the older series all the way up through whatever I'm doing by December of this year, and pick and choose. I'll have various series spiraling the ramp. Dia was one subject in depth. This new installation will be more across-the-board, which I think will be suitable for a museum audience. The writing won't be about art and museums, and it won't be about me, at least directly.

DW: I have read that a cross-section of your work will be shown in Venice next year. I know that you haven't come to any decisions about Venice, but I wonder if you can discuss what you are thinking about for the *Biennale*?

JH: I'm thinking that various public projects outside the American Pavilion might be good places for a retrospective or selection of earlier work. Inside the pavilion I will do something new. I have some ideas about the installation. I like the delicate lines, the fine stripes of color in Venetian glass. So in some of the galleries I might make bands of light with LED signs. In one space I would have horizontals wrapping the room so that there would be bands all around, and then have skinny vertical signs in another room. You will completely lose the space; there will just be lines of light. I also am considering redoing the floors—rather than having a lot of stone objects, I would lay the stone on the floor and have inscriptions there. The materials would melt away.

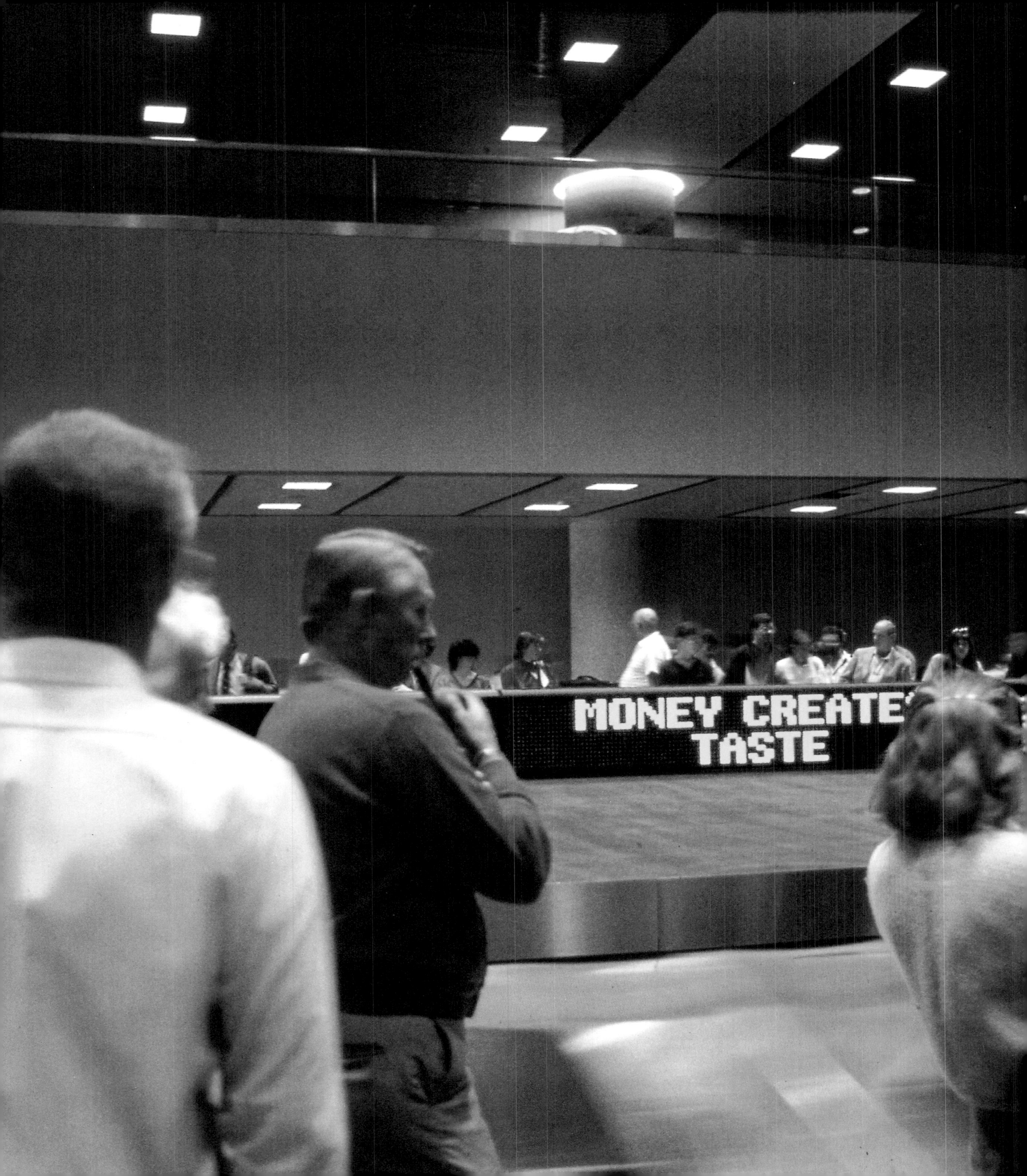
MONEY CREATES
TASTE

opposite: From *Truisms*. Electronic sign, 8 x 13 feet. Installation, baggage carousel, McCarran International Airport, Las Vegas, 1986. Organized by Nevada Institute of Contemporary Art, University of Nevada, Las Vegas.

A LITTLE KNOWLEDGE CAN GO A LONG WAY

A LOT OF PROFESSIONALS ARE CRACKPOTS

A MAN CAN'T KNOW WHAT IT'S LIKE TO BE A MOTHER

A NAME MEANS A LOT JUST BY ITSELF

A POSITIVE ATTITUDE MAKES ALL THE DIFFERENCE IN THE WORLD

A RELAXED MAN IS NOT NECESSARILY A BETTER MAN

A SENSE OF TIMING IS THE MARK OF GENIUS

A SINCERE EFFORT IS ALL YOU CAN ASK

A SINGLE EVENT CAN HAVE INFINITELY MANY INTERPRETATIONS

A SOLID HOME BASE BUILDS A SENSE OF SELF

A STRONG SENSE OF DUTY IMPRISONS YOU

ABSOLUTE SUBMISSION CAN BE A FORM OF FREEDOM

ABSTRACTION IS A TYPE OF DECADENCE

ABUSE OF POWER COMES AS NO SURPRISE

ACTION CAUSES MORE TROUBLE THAN THOUGHT

ALIENATION PRODUCES ECCENTRICS OR REVOLUTIONARIES

ALL THINGS ARE DELICATELY INTERCONNECTED

AMBITION IS JUST AS DANGEROUS AS COMPLACENCY

AMBIVALENCE CAN RUIN YOUR LIFE

AN ELITE IS INEVITABLE

ANGER OR HATE CAN BE A USEFUL MOTIVATING FORCE

ANIMALISM IS PERFECTLY HEALTHY

ANY SURPLUS IS IMMORAL

ANYTHING IS A LEGITIMATE AREA OF INVESTIGATION

ARTIFICIAL DESIRES ARE DESPOILING THE EARTH

AT TIMES INACTIVITY IS PREFERABLE TO MINDLESS FUNCTIONING

AT TIMES YOUR UNCONSCIOUS IS TRUER THAN YOUR CONSCIOUS MIND

AUTOMATION IS DEADLY

AWFUL PUNISHMENT AWAITS REALLY BAD PEOPLE

BAD INTENTIONS CAN YIELD GOOD RESULTS

BEING ALONE WITH YOURSELF IS INCREASINGLY UNPOPULAR

BEING HAPPY IS MORE IMPORTANT THAN ANYTHING ELSE

BEING JUDGMENTAL IS A SIGN OF LIFE

BEING SURE OF YOURSELF MEANS YOU'RE A FOOL

BELIEVING IN REBIRTH IS THE SAME AS ADMITTING DEFEAT

BOREDOM MAKES YOU DO CRAZY THINGS

CALM IS MORE CONDUCIVE TO CREATIVITY THAN IS ANXIETY

CATEGORIZING FEAR IS CALMING

CHANGE IS VALUABLE WHEN THE OPPRESSED BECOME TYRANTS

CHASING THE NEW IS DANGEROUS TO SOCIETY

CHILDREN ARE THE HOPE OF THE FUTURE

CHILDREN ARE THE MOST CRUEL OF ALL

CLASS ACTION IS A NICE IDEA WITH NO SUBSTANCE

CLASS STRUCTURE IS AS ARTIFICIAL AS PLASTIC

CONFUSING YOURSELF IS A WAY TO STAY HONEST

CRIME AGAINST PROPERTY IS RELATIVELY UNIMPORTANT

DECADENCE CAN BE AN END IN ITSELF

DECENCY IS A RELATIVE THING

DEPENDENCE CAN BE A MEAL TICKET

DESCRIPTION IS MORE VALUABLE THAN METAPHOR

DEVIANTS ARE SACRIFICED TO INCREASE GROUP SOLIDARITY

DISGUST IS THE APPROPRIATE RESPONSE TO MOST SITUATIONS

DISORGANIZATION IS A KIND OF ANESTHESIA

DON'T PLACE TOO MUCH TRUST IN EXPERTS

DRAMA OFTEN OBSCURES THE REAL ISSUES

DREAMING WHILE AWAKE IS A FRIGHTENING CONTRADICTION

DYING AND COMING BACK GIVES YOU CONSIDERABLE PERSPECTIVE

DYING SHOULD BE AS EASY AS FALLING OFF A LOG

EATING TOO MUCH IS CRIMINAL

ELABORATION IS A FORM OF POLLUTION

EMOTIONAL RESPONSES ARE AS VALUABLE AS INTELLECTUAL RESPONSES

ENJOY YOURSELF BECAUSE YOU CAN'T CHANGE ANYTHING ANYWAY

ENSURE THAT YOUR LIFE STAYS IN FLUX

EVEN YOUR FAMILY CAN BETRAY YOU

EVERY ACHIEVEMENT REQUIRES A SACRIFICE

EVERYONE'S WORK IS EQUALLY IMPORTANT

EVERYTHING THAT'S INTERESTING IS NEW

EXCEPTIONAL PEOPLE DESERVE SPECIAL CONCESSIONS

EXPIRING FOR LOVE IS BEAUTIFUL BUT STUPID

EXPRESSING ANGER IS NECESSARY

EXTREME BEHAVIOR HAS ITS BASIS IN PATHOLOGICAL PSYCHOLOGY

EXTREME SELF-CONSCIOUSNESS LEADS TO PERVERSION

FAITHFULNESS IS A SOCIAL NOT A BIOLOGICAL LAW

FAKE OR REAL INDIFFERENCE IS A POWERFUL PERSONAL WEAPON

FATHERS OFTEN USE TOO MUCH FORCE

FEAR IS THE GREATEST INCAPACITATOR

FREEDOM IS A LUXURY NOT A NECESSITY

GIVING FREE REIN TO YOUR EMOTIONS IS AN HONEST WAY TO LIVE

GO ALL OUT IN ROMANCE AND LET THE CHIPS FALL WHERE THEY MAY

GOING WITH THE FLOW IS SOOTHING BUT RISKY

GOOD DEEDS EVENTUALLY ARE REWARDED

GOVERNMENT IS A BURDEN ON THE PEOPLE

GRASS ROOTS AGITATION IS THE ONLY HOPE

GUILT AND SELF-LACERATION ARE INDULGENCES

HABITUAL CONTEMPT DOESN'T REFLECT A FINER SENSIBILITY

HIDING YOUR EMOTIONS IS DESPICABLE

HOLDING BACK PROTECTS YOUR VITAL ENERGIES

HUMANISM IS OBSOLETE

HUMOR IS A RELEASE

IDEALS ARE REPLACED BY CONVENTIONAL GOALS AT A CERTAIN AGE

IF YOU AREN'T POLITICAL YOUR PERSONAL LIFE SHOULD BE EXEMPLARY

IF YOU CAN'T LEAVE YOUR MARK GIVE UP

IF YOU HAVE MANY DESIRES YOUR LIFE WILL BE INTERESTING

IF YOU LIVE SIMPLY THERE IS NOTHING TO WORRY ABOUT

IGNORING ENEMIES IS THE BEST WAY TO FIGHT

ILLNESS IS A STATE OF MIND

IMPOSING ORDER IS MAN'S VOCATION FOR CHAOS IS HELL

IN SOME INSTANCES IT'S BETTER TO DIE THAN TO CONTINUE

INHERITANCE MUST BE ABOLISHED

IT CAN BE HELPFUL TO KEEP GOING NO MATTER WHAT

IT IS HEROIC TO TRY TO STOP TIME

IT IS MAN'S FATE TO OUTSMART HIMSELF

IT'S A GIFT TO THE WORLD NOT TO HAVE BABIES

IT'S BETTER TO BE A GOOD PERSON THAN A FAMOUS PERSON

IT'S BETTER TO BE LONELY THAN TO BE WITH INFERIOR PEOPLE

IT'S BETTER TO BE NAIVE THAN JADED

IT'S BETTER TO STUDY THE LIVING FACT THAN TO ANALYZE HISTORY

IT'S CRUCIAL TO HAVE AN ACTIVE FANTASY LIFE

IT'S GOOD TO GIVE EXTRA MONEY TO CHARITY

IT'S IMPORTANT TO STAY CLEAN ON ALL LEVELS

IT'S JUST AN ACCIDENT THAT YOUR PARENTS ARE YOUR PARENTS

IT'S NOT GOOD TO HOLD TOO MANY ABSOLUTES

IT'S NOT GOOD TO OPERATE ON CREDIT

IT'S VITAL TO LIVE IN HARMONY WITH NATURE

JUST BELIEVING SOMETHING CAN MAKE IT HAPPEN

KEEP SOMETHING IN RESERVE FOR EMERGENCIES

KILLING IS UNAVOIDABLE BUT IS NOTHING TO BE PROUD OF

KNOWING YOURSELF LETS YOU UNDERSTAND OTHERS

KNOWLEDGE SHOULD BE ADVANCED AT ALL COSTS

LABOR IS A LIFE-DESTROYING ACTIVITY

LACK OF CHARISMA CAN BE FATAL

LEISURE TIME IS A GIGANTIC SMOKE SCREEN

LISTEN WHEN YOUR BODY TALKS

LOOKING BACK IS THE FIRST SIGN OF AGING AND DECAY

LOVING ANIMALS IS A SUBSTITUTE ACTIVITY

LOW EXPECTATIONS ARE GOOD PROTECTION

MANUAL LABOR CAN BE REFRESHING AND WHOLESOME

MEN ARE NOT MONOGAMOUS BY NATURE

MODERATION KILLS THE SPIRIT

MONEY CREATES TASTE

MONOMANIA IS A PREREQUISITE OF SUCCESS

MORALS ARE FOR LITTLE PEOPLE

MOST PEOPLE ARE NOT FIT TO RULE THEMSELVES

MOSTLY YOU SHOULD MIND YOUR OWN BUSINESS

MOTHERS SHOULDN'T MAKE TOO MANY SACRIFICES

MUCH WAS DECIDED BEFORE YOU WERE BORN

MURDER HAS ITS SEXUAL SIDE

MYTHS CAN MAKE REALITY MORE INTELLIGIBLE

NOISE CAN BE HOSTILE

NOTHING UPSETS THE BALANCE OF GOOD AND EVIL

OCCASIONALLY PRINCIPLES ARE MORE VALUABLE THAN PEOPLE

OFFER VERY LITTLE INFORMATION ABOUT YOURSELF

OFTEN YOU SHOULD ACT LIKE YOU ARE SEXLESS

OLD FRIENDS ARE BETTER LEFT IN THE PAST

OPACITY IS AN IRRESISTIBLE CHALLENGE

PAIN CAN BE A VERY POSITIVE THING

PEOPLE ARE BORING UNLESS THEY'RE EXTREMISTS

PEOPLE ARE NUTS IF THEY THINK THEY ARE IMPORTANT

PEOPLE ARE RESPONSIBLE FOR WHAT THEY DO UNLESS THEY'RE INSANE

PEOPLE WHO DON'T WORK WITH THEIR HANDS ARE PARASITES

PEOPLE WHO GO CRAZY ARE TOO SENSITIVE

PEOPLE WON'T BEHAVE IF THEY HAVE NOTHING TO LOSE

PHYSICAL CULTURE IS SECOND-BEST

PLANNING FOR THE FUTURE IS ESCAPISM

PLAYING IT SAFE CAN CAUSE A LOT OF DAMAGE IN THE LONG RUN

POLITICS IS USED FOR PERSONAL GAIN

POTENTIAL COUNTS FOR NOTHING UNTIL IT'S REALIZED

PRIVATE PROPERTY CREATED CRIME

PURSUING PLEASURE FOR THE SAKE OF PLEASURE WILL RUIN YOU

PUSH YOURSELF TO THE LIMIT AS OFTEN AS POSSIBLE

RAISE BOYS AND GIRLS THE SAME WAY

RANDOM MATING IS GOOD FOR DEBUNKING SEX MYTHS

RECHANNELING DESTRUCTIVE IMPULSES IS A SIGN OF MATURITY

RECLUSES ALWAYS GET WEAK

REDISTRIBUTING WEALTH IS IMPERATIVE

RELATIVITY IS NO BOON TO MANKIND

RELIGION CAUSES AS MANY PROBLEMS AS IT SOLVES

REMEMBER YOU ALWAYS HAVE FREEDOM OF CHOICE

REPETITION IS THE BEST WAY TO LEARN

RESOLUTIONS SERVE TO EASE YOUR CONSCIENCE

REVOLUTION BEGINS WITH CHANGES IN THE INDIVIDUAL

ROMANTIC LOVE WAS INVENTED TO MANIPULATE WOMEN

ROUTINE IS A LINK WITH THE PAST

ROUTINE SMALL EXCESSES ARE WORSE THAN THE OCCASIONAL DEBAUCH

SACRIFICING YOURSELF FOR A BAD CAUSE IS NOT A MORAL ACT

SALVATION CAN'T BE BOUGHT AND SOLD

SELF-AWARENESS CAN BE CRIPPLING

SELF-CONTEMPT CAN DO MORE HARM THAN GOOD

SELFISHNESS IS THE MOST BASIC MOTIVATION

SELFLESSNESS IS THE HIGHEST ACHIEVEMENT

SEPARATISM IS THE WAY TO A NEW BEGINNING

SEX DIFFERENCES ARE HERE TO STAY

SIN IS A MEANS OF SOCIAL CONTROL

SLIPPING INTO MADNESS IS GOOD FOR THE SAKE OF COMPARISON

SLOPPY THINKING GETS WORSE OVER TIME

SOLITUDE IS ENRICHING

SOMETIMES SCIENCE ADVANCES FASTER THAN IT SHOULD

SOMETIMES THINGS SEEM TO HAPPEN OF THEIR OWN ACCORD

SPENDING TOO MUCH TIME ON SELF-IMPROVEMENT IS ANTISOCIAL

STARVATION IS NATURE'S WAY

STASIS IS A DREAM STATE

STERILIZATION IS A WEAPON OF THE RULERS

STRONG EMOTIONAL ATTACHMENT STEMS FROM BASIC INSECURITY

STUPID PEOPLE SHOULDN'T BREED

SURVIVAL OF THE FITTEST APPLIES TO MEN AND ANIMALS

SYMBOLS ARE MORE MEANINGFUL THAN THINGS THEMSELVES

TAKING A STRONG STAND PUBLICIZES THE OPPOSITE POSITION

TALKING IS USED TO HIDE ONE'S INABILITY TO ACT

TEASING PEOPLE SEXUALLY CAN HAVE UGLY CONSEQUENCES

TECHNOLOGY WILL MAKE OR BREAK US

THE CRUELEST DISAPPOINTMENT IS WHEN YOU LET YOURSELF DOWN

THE DESIRE TO REPRODUCE IS A DEATH WISH

THE FAMILY IS LIVING ON BORROWED TIME

THE IDEA OF REVOLUTION IS AN ADOLESCENT FANTASY

THE IDEA OF TRANSCENDENCE IS USED TO OBSCURE OPPRESSION

THE IDIOSYNCRATIC HAS LOST ITS AUTHORITY

THE MOST PROFOUND THINGS ARE INEXPRESSIBLE

THE MUNDANE IS TO BE CHERISHED

THE NEW IS NOTHING BUT A RESTATEMENT OF THE OLD

THE ONLY WAY TO BE PURE IS TO STAY BY YOURSELF

THE SUM OF YOUR ACTIONS DETERMINES WHAT YOU ARE

THE UNATTAINABLE IS INVARIABLY ATTRACTIVE

THE WORLD OPERATES ACCORDING TO DISCOVERABLE LAWS

THERE ARE TOO FEW IMMUTABLE TRUTHS TODAY

THERE'S NOTHING EXCEPT WHAT YOU SENSE

THERE'S NOTHING REDEEMING IN TOIL

THINKING TOO MUCH CAN ONLY CAUSE PROBLEMS

THREATENING SOMEONE SEXUALLY IS A HORRIBLE ACT

TIMIDITY IS LAUGHABLE

TO DISAGREE PRESUPPOSES MORAL INTEGRITY

TO VOLUNTEER IS REACTIONARY

TORTURE IS BARBARIC

TRADING A LIFE FOR A LIFE IS FAIR ENOUGH

TRUE FREEDOM IS FRIGHTFUL

UNIQUE THINGS MUST BE THE MOST VALUABLE

UNQUESTIONING LOVE DEMONSTRATES LARGESSE OF SPIRIT

USING FORCE TO STOP FORCE IS ABSURD

VIOLENCE IS PERMISSIBLE EVEN DESIRABLE OCCASIONALLY

WAR IS A PURIFICATION RITE

WE MUST MAKE SACRIFICES TO MAINTAIN OUR QUALITY OF LIFE

WHEN SOMETHING TERRIBLE HAPPENS PEOPLE WAKE UP

WISHING THINGS AWAY IS NOT EFFECTIVE

WITH PERSEVERANCE YOU CAN DISCOVER ANY TRUTH

WORDS TEND TO BE INADEQUATE

WORRYING CAN HELP YOU PREPARE

YOU ARE A VICTIM OF THE RULES YOU LIVE BY

YOU ARE GUILELESS IN YOUR DREAMS

YOU ARE RESPONSIBLE FOR CONSTITUTING THE MEANING OF THINGS

YOU ARE THE PAST PRESENT AND FUTURE

YOU CAN LIVE ON THROUGH YOUR DESCENDANTS

YOU CAN'T EXPECT PEOPLE TO BE SOMETHING THEY'RE NOT

YOU CAN'T FOOL OTHERS IF YOU'RE FOOLING YOURSELF

YOU DON'T KNOW WHAT'S WHAT UNTIL YOU SUPPORT YOURSELF

YOU HAVE TO HURT OTHERS TO BE EXTRAORDINARY

YOU MUST BE INTIMATE WITH A TOKEN FEW

YOU MUST DISAGREE WITH AUTHORITY FIGURES

YOU MUST HAVE ONE GRAND PASSION

YOU MUST KNOW WHERE YOU STOP AND THE WORLD BEGINS

YOU ONLY CAN UNDERSTAND SOMEONE OF YOUR OWN SEX

YOU OWE THE WORLD NOT THE OTHER WAY AROUND

YOU SHOULD STUDY AS MUCH AS POSSIBLE

YOUR ACTIONS ARE POINTLESS IF NO ONE NOTICES

YOUR OLDEST FEARS ARE THE WORST ONES

opposite: From *Truisms* (in Spanish and English). Color photostats and audiotape; photostats: 8 feet x 36 inches each. Installation, Fashion Moda window, Bronx, 1979. Organized by Fashion Moda.

pages 46–47: From *Truisms*. Double-sided silver photostats, 8 feet x 36 inches each. Installation, Marine Midland Bank lobby, 140 Broadway, New York, 1982. Organized by Lower Manhattan Cultural Council, New York.

ON IS THE ONLY HOPE
ARE INDULGENCES
DOESN'T REFLECT A FINER SENSIBILITY
A CERTAIN AGE
OULD BE EXEMPLARY
ORRY ABOUT
THE WHOLE
IT'S VITAL TO LIVE IN HARMONY WITH NATURE
JUST BELIEVING IN SOMETHING CAN MAKE IT HAPPEN
KEEP SOMETHING IN RESERVE FOR EMERGENCIES
KILLING IS UNAVOIDABLE BUT IS NOTHING TO BE PROUD OF
KNOWING YOURSELF LETS YOU UNDERSTAND OTHERS
KNOWLEDGE SHOULD BE ADVANCED AT ALL COSTS
IS A LIFE-DESTROYING ACTIVITY
CHARISMA CAN BE FATAL
GS FROM THE GROUND UP
RUST YOUR OWN EYES
E IS A GIGANTIC SMOKESCREEN
O IS THE HARDEST THING TO DO
HEN YOUR BODY TALKS
ACK IS THE FIRST SIGN OF AGING AND DECAY
IS A SUBSTITUTE ACTIVITY
PROTECTION
G AND WHOLESOME
ATURE
UCCESS

above and opposite: From
Truisms. Spectacolor
electronic sign, 20 x
40 feet. Installation, Times
Square, New York, 1982.
Organized by Public Art
Fund, Inc., New York.

following two pages: From
Truisms. T-shirts. Worn by
Lady Pink, New York, 1983,
and John Ahearn, New
York, 1982.

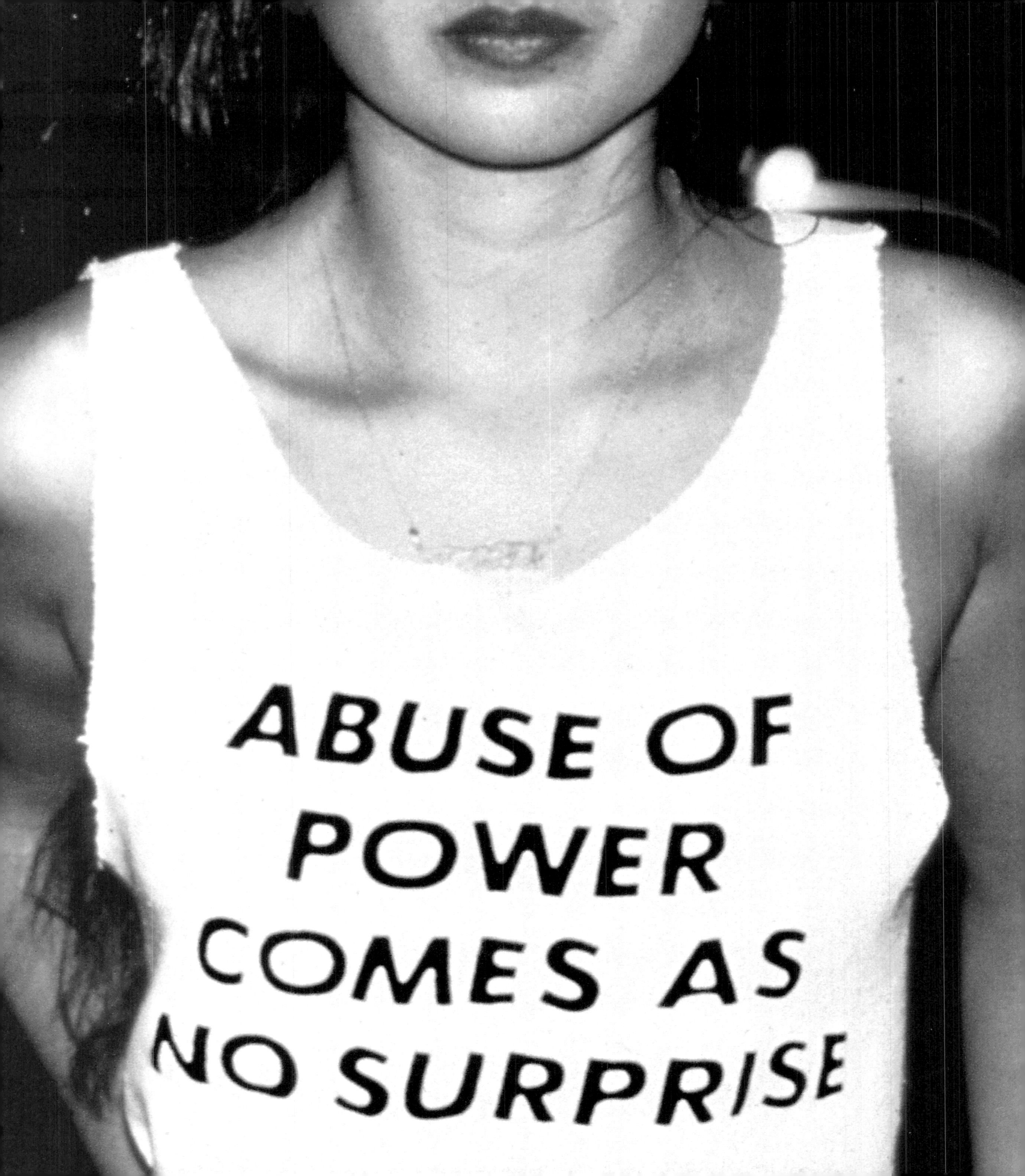
ABUSE OF
POWER
COMES AS
NO SURPRISE

ABUSE OF POWER SHOULD COME AS NO SURPRISE
ALIENATION CAN PRODUCE ECCENTRICS OR REVOLUTIONARIES
AN ELITE IS INEVITABLE
ANGER OR HATE CAN BE A USEFUL MOTIVATING FORCE
ANY SURPLUS IS IMMORAL
DISGUST IS THE APPROPRIATE RESPONSE TO MOST SITUATIONS
EVERYONE'S WORK IS EQUALLY IMPORTANT
EXCEPTIONAL PEOPLE DESERVE SPECIAL CONCESSIONS
FAITHFULNESS IS A SOCIAL NOT A BIOLOGICAL LAW
FREEDOM IS A LUXURY NOT A NECESSITY
GOVERNMENT IS A BURDEN ON THE PEOPLE
HUMANISM IS OBSOLETE
IDEALS ARE EVENTUALLY REPLACED BY CONVENTIONAL GOALS
INHERITANCE MUST BE ABOLISHED
KILLING IS UNAVOIDABLE BUT IS NOTHING TO BE PROUD OF
LABOR IS A LIFE-DESTROYING ACTIVITY
MONEY CREATES TASTE
MORALS ARE FOR LITTLE PEOPLE
MOST PEOPLE ARE NOT FIT TO RULE THEMSELVES
MOSTLY YOU SHOULD MIND YOUR OWN BUSINESS
MUCH WAS DECIDED BEFORE YOU WERE BORN
MURDER HAS ITS SEXUAL SIDE
PAIN CAN BE A VERY POSITIVE THING
PEOPLE ARE NUTS IF THEY THINK THEY CONTROL THEIR LIVES
PEOPLE WHO DON'T WORK WITH THEIR HANDS ARE PARASITES
PEOPLE WHO GO CRAZY ARE TOO SENSITIVE
PEOPLE WON'T BEHAVE IF THEY HAVE NOTHING TO LOSE
PLAYING IT SAFE CAN CAUSE A LOT OF DAMAGE
PRIVATE OWNERSHIP IS AN INVITATION TO DISASTER
ROMANTIC LOVE WAS INVENTED TO MANIPULATE WOMEN
SELFISHNESS IS THE MOST BASIC MOTIVATION
SEPARATISM IS THE WAY TO A NEW BEGINNING
SEX DIFFERENCES ARE HERE TO STAY

From *Truisms*. Daktronics double-sided electronic sign, 20 x 40 feet. Installation, Caesars Palace, Las Vegas, 1986. Organized by Nevada Institute of Contemporary Art, University of Nevada, Las Vegas.

From *Truisms*. Electronic
sign, 15 x 60 feet.
Installation, Showplace
Square, San Francisco,
1987. Organized by
Artspace, San Francisco.

opposite: From *Truisms*.
Sony JumboTRON
video sign, 24 x 32 feet.
Installation, Candlestick
Park, San Francisco, 1987.
Organized by Artspace,
San Francisco.

pages 56–57: From
Truisms and *Under a Rock*.
Danby Royal marble and
Misty Black granite
benches, 17 x 54 x
25 inches (Danby Royal),
17 ¼ x 48 x 21 inches
(Misty Black) each.
Installation, Doris C.
Freedman Plaza, New
York, 1989. Organized
by Public Art Fund, Inc.,
New York.

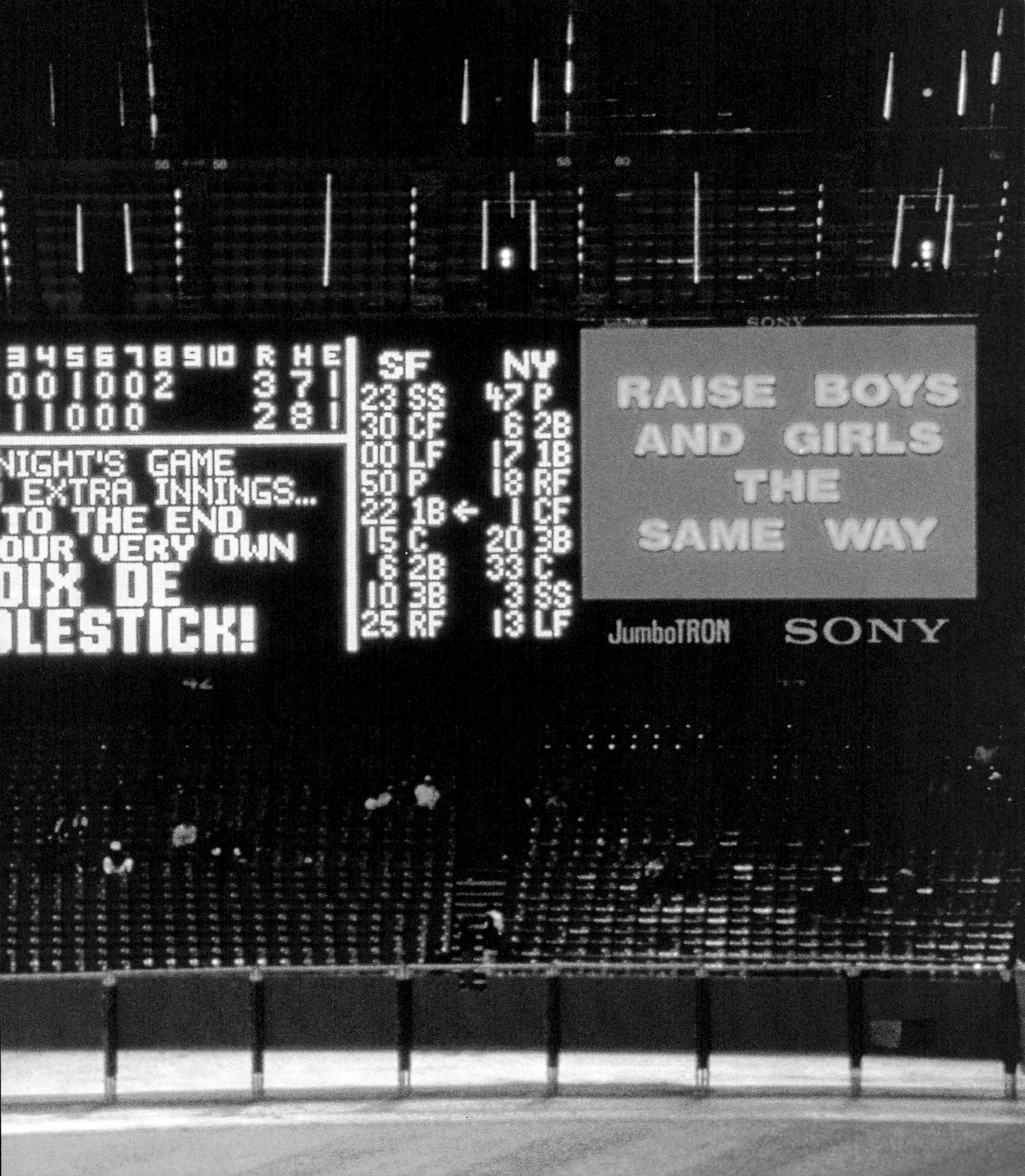
3 4 5 6 7 8 9 10 R H E
0 0 1 0 0 2 3 7 1
1 1 0 0 0 2 8 1
NIGHT'S GAME
EXTRA INNINGS...
TO THE END
OUR VERY OWN
DIX DE
OLESTICK!
SF NY
23 SS 47 P
30 CF 6 2B
00 LF 17 1B
50 P 18 RF
22 1B 1 CF
15 C 20 3B
6 2B 33 C
10 3B 3 SS
25 RF 13 LF
RAISE BOYS AND GIRLS THE SAME WAY
JumboTRON
SONY

From *Truisms*. Maiden Spectacolor electronic sign, 15 x 30 feet. Installation, Piccadilly Circus, London, 1988–89. Organized by The Artangel Trust, London.

From *Truisms*. Daktronics electronic sign, 64 x 128 feet. Installation, Pilot Field, Buffalo, 1991. Organized by Albright-Knox Art Gallery, Buffalo.

following two pages: From *Truisms*. Theater marquee; front: approx. 8 feet 6 inches x 18 feet; side: approx. 8 feet 6 inches x 19 feet. Installation, Forty-second Street, New York, 1993. Organized by Creative Time, New York.

DON'T TALK DOWN TO ME. DON'T
BE POLITE TO ME. DON'T
TRY TO MAKE ME FEEL NICE.
DON'T RELAX. I'LL CUT THE
SMILE OFF YOUR FACE. YOU
THINK I DON'T KNOW WHAT'S
GOING ON. YOU THINK I'M
AFRAID TO REACT. THE JOKE'S
ON YOU. I'M BIDING MY TIME,
LOOKING FOR THE SPOT. YOU
THINK NO ONE CAN REACH YOU,
NO ONE CAN HAVE WHAT YOU
HAVE. I'VE BEEN PLANNING
WHILE YOU'RE PLAYING. I'VE
BEEN SAVING WHILE YOU'RE
SPENDING. THE GAME IS
ALMOST OVER SO IT'S
TIME YOU ACKNOWLEDGE ME.
DO YOU WANT TO FALL NOT
EVER KNOWING WHO TOOK YOU?

opposite: From *Inflammatory Essays*. Offset print on paper with graffiti, 17 x 17 inches. Street installation, New York, 1982.

A CRUEL BUT ANCIENT LAW DEMANDS AN EYE FOR AN EYE. MURDER MUST BE ANSWERED BY EXECUTION. ONLY GOD HAS THE RIGHT TO TAKE A LIFE AND WHEN SOMEONE BREAKS THIS LAW HE WILL BE PUNISHED. JUSTICE MUST COME SWIFTLY. IT DOESN'T HELP ANYONE TO STALL. THE VICTIM'S FAMILY CRIES OUT FOR SATISFACTION, THE COMMUNITY BEGS FOR PROTECTION AND THE DEPARTED CRAVES VENGEANCE SO HE CAN REST. THE KILLER KNEW IN ADVANCE THERE WAS NO EXCUSE FOR HIS ACT. TRULY HE HAS TAKEN HIS OWN LIFE. HE, NOT SOCIETY, IS RESPONSIBLE FOR HIS FATE. HE ALONE STANDS GUILTY AND DAMNED.

A REAL TORTURE WOULD BE TO BUILD A SPARKLING CAGE WITH TWO-WAY MIRRORS AND STEEL BARS. IN THERE WOULD BE GOOD-LOOKING AND YOUNG GIRLS WHO'LL THINK THEY'RE IN A REGULAR MOTEL ROOM SO THEY'LL TAKE THEIR CLOTHES OFF AND DO THE DELICATE THINGS THAT GIRLS DO WHEN THEY'RE ALONE. EVERYONE WHO WATCHES WILL GO CRAZY BECAUSE THEY WON'T BE BELIEVING WHAT THEY'RE SEEING BUT THEY'LL SEE THE BARS AND KNOW THEY CAN'T GET IN, AND THEY'LL BE AFRAID TO MAKE A MOVE BECAUSE THEY DON'T WANT TO SCARE THE GIRLS AWAY FROM DOING THE DELICIOUS THINGS THEY'RE DOING.

BECAUSE THERE IS NO GOD SOMEONE MUST TAKE RESPONSIBILITY FOR MEN. A CHARISMATIC LEADER IS IMPERATIVE. HE CAN SUBORDINATE THE SMALL WILLS TO THE GREAT ONE. HIS STRENGTH AND HIS VISION REDEEM MEN. HIS PERFECTION MAKES THEM GRATEFUL. LIFE ITSELF IS NOT SACRED, THERE IS NO DIGNITY IN THE FLESH. UNDIRECTED MEN ARE CONTENT WITH RANDOM, SQUALID, POINTLESS LIVES. THE LEADER GIVES DIRECTION AND PURPOSE. THE LEADER FORCES GREAT ACCOMPLISHMENTS, MANDATES PEACE AND REPELS OUTSIDE AGGRESSORS. HE IS THE ARCHITECT OF DESTINY. HE DEMANDS ABSOLUTE LOYALTY. HE MERITS UNQUESTIONING DEVOTION. HE ASKS THE SUPREME SACRIFICE. HE IS THE ONLY HOPE.

CHANGE IS THE BASIS OF ALL HISTORY, THE PROOF OF VIGOR. THE OLD IS SOILED AND DISGUSTING BY NATURE. STALE FOOD IS REPELLENT, MONOGAMOUS LOVE BREEDS CONTEMPT, SENILITY CRIPPLES THE GOVERNMENT THAT IS TOO POWERFUL TOO LONG. UPHEAVAL IS DESIRABLE BECAUSE FRESH, UNTAINTED GROUPS SEIZE OPPORTUNITY. VIOLENT OVERTHROW IS APPROPRIATE WHEN THE SITUATION IS INTOLERABLE. SLOW MODIFICATION CAN BE EFFECTIVE; MEN CHANGE BEFORE THEY NOTICE AND RESIST. THE DECADENT AND THE POWERFUL CHAMPION CONTINUITY. "NOTHING ESSENTIAL CHANGES." THAT IS A MYTH. IT WILL BE REFUTED. THE NECESSARY BIRTH CONVULSIONS WILL BE TRIGGERED. ACTION WILL BRING THE EVIDENCE TO YOUR DOORSTEP.

CHILD MOLESTATION IS ABHORRENT; THIS DEVIATION IS UNIVERSALLY CONDEMNED. ALL PEOPLE ARE SICKENED AND ENRAGED BY THE ACT. IT IS TELLING THAT PRISONERS, WHO ARE NOT KNOWN FOR THEIR HIGH STANDARDS, OSTRACIZE AND KILL CHILD MOLESTERS. NO PUNISHMENT IS TOO SEVERE; CHILD MOLESTERS HAVE ROBBED THE BABIES OF THEIR INNOCENCE, THE MOST PRECIOUS POSSESSION OF CHILDHOOD. MOLESTATION LEAVES SPIRITUAL, EMOTIONAL AND PHYSICAL WOUNDS THAT MAY NEVER HEAL. THE FRIGHTENING ASPECT OF THE ABUSE IS THAT MOLESTED CHILDREN OFTEN BECOME CHILD MOLESTERS. THE AWFUL CYCLE MUST BE STOPPED BEFORE ANY MORE CHILDREN ARE DEFILED AND RUINED. MOLESTERS SHOULD BE RENDERED IMPOTENT.

DESTROY SUPERABUNDANCE. STARVE THE FLESH, SHAVE THE HAIR, EXPOSE THE BONE, CLARIFY THE MIND, DEFINE THE WILL, RESTRAIN THE SENSES, LEAVE THE FAMILY, FLEE THE CHURCH, KILL THE VERMIN, VOMIT THE HEART, FORGET THE DEAD. LIMIT TIME, FORGO AMUSEMENT, DENY NATURE, REJECT ACQUAINTANCES, DISCARD OBJECTS, FORGET TRUTHS, DISSECT MYTH, STOP MOTION, BLOCK IMPULSE, CHOKE SOBS, SWALLOW CHATTER. SCORN JOY, SCORN TOUCH, SCORN TRAGEDY, SCORN LIBERTY, SCORN CONSTANCY, SCORN HOPE, SCORN EXALTATION, SCORN REPRODUCTION, SCORN VARIETY, SCORN EMBELLISHMENT, SCORN RELEASE, SCORN REST, SCORN SWEETNESS, SCORN THE LIGHT. IT IS A QUESTION OF FORM AND FUNCTION. IT IS A MATTER OF REVULSION.

DON'T TALK DOWN TO ME.
DON'T BE POLITE TO ME. DON'T
TRY TO MAKE ME FEEL NICE.
DON'T RELAX. I'LL CUT THE
SMILE OFF YOUR FACE. YOU
THINK I DON'T KNOW WHAT'S
GOING ON. YOU THINK I'M
AFRAID TO REACT. THE JOKE'S
ON YOU. I'M BIDING MY TIME,
LOOKING FOR THE SPOT. YOU
THINK NO ONE CAN REACH
YOU, NO ONE CAN HAVE WHAT
YOU HAVE. I'VE BEEN PLANNING
WHILE YOU'RE PLAYING. I'VE
BEEN SAVING WHILE YOU'RE
SPENDING. THE GAME IS ALMOST
OVER SO IT'S TIME YOU
ACKNOWLEDGE ME. DO YOU
WANT TO FALL NOT EVER
KNOWING WHO TOOK YOU?

FEAR IS THE MOST ELEGANT WEAPON.
YOUR HANDS ARE NEVER MESSY.
THREATENING BODILY HARM IS CRUDE.
WORK INSTEAD ON MINDS AND BELIEFS,
PLAY INSECURITIES LIKE A PIANO. BE
CREATIVE IN APPROACH. FORCE ANXIETY
TO EXCRUCIATING LEVELS OR GENTLY
UNDERMINE THE PUBLIC CONFIDENCE.
PANIC DRIVES HUMAN HERDS OVER
CLIFFS; AN ALTERNATIVE IS TERROR-
INDUCED IMMOBILIZATION. FEAR FEEDS
ON FEAR. PUT THIS EFFICIENT PROCESS IN
MOTION. MANIPULATION IS NOT LIMITED
TO PEOPLE. ECONOMIC, SOCIAL AND
DEMOCRATIC INSTITUTIONS CAN BE
SHAKEN. IT WILL BE DEMONSTRATED
THAT NOTHING IS SAFE, SACRED OR SANE.
THERE IS NO RESPITE FROM HORROR.
ABSOLUTES ARE QUICKSILVER. RESULTS
ARE SPECTACULAR.

FREEDOM IS IT! YOU'RE SO SCARED,
YOU WANT TO LOCK UP EVERYBODY.
ARE THEY MAD DOGS? ARE THEY
OUT TO KILL? MAYBE YES. IS LAW, IS
ORDER THE SOLUTION? DEFINITELY
NO. WHAT CAUSED THIS SITUATION?
LACK OF FREEDOM. WHAT HAPPENS
NOW? LET PEOPLE FULFILL THEIR
NEEDS. IS FREEDOM CONSTRUCTIVE
OR IS IT DESTRUCTIVE? THE ANSWER
IS OBVIOUS. FREE PEOPLE ARE
GOOD, PRODUCTIVE PEOPLE. IS
LIBERATION DANGEROUS? ONLY
WHEN OVERDUE. PEOPLE AREN'T
BORN RABID OR BERSERK. WHEN
YOU PUNISH AND SHAME YOU
CAUSE WHAT YOU DREAD. WHAT
TO DO? LET IT EXPLODE. RUN WITH
IT. DON'T CONTROL OR MANIPULATE.
MAKE AMENDS.

IT ALL HAS TO BURN, IT'S GOING
TO BLAZE. IT IS FILTHY AND CAN'T
BE SAVED. A COUPLE OF GOOD
THINGS WILL BURN WITH THE REST
BUT IT'S O.K., EVERY PIECE IS PART
OF THE UGLY WHOLE. EVERYTHING
CONSPIRES TO KEEP YOU HUNGRY
AND AFRAID FOR YOUR BABIES.
DON'T WAIT ANY LONGER.
WAITING IS WEAKNESS, WEAKNESS
IS SLAVERY. BURN DOWN THE
SYSTEM THAT HAS NO PLACE FOR
YOU, RISE TRIUMPHANT FROM THE
ASHES. FIRE PURIFIES AND
RELEASES ENERGY. FIRE GIVES
HEAT AND LIGHT. LET FIRE BE THE
CELEBRATION OF YOUR
DELIVERANCE. LET LIGHTNING
STRIKE, LET THE FLAMES DEVOUR
THE ENEMY!

MONDAY, SOMEONE DIED BECAUSE
HE HURT ME AND I CUT HIM
WITHOUT THINKING. TUESDAY,
SOME ANIMAL DIED BECAUSE HE
WAS TOO DANGEROUS TO BE FREE.
WEDNESDAY, A THIEF DIED SO
EVERYONE WILL KNOW TO RESPECT
PRIVATE PROPERTY. THURSDAY,
SOME POLITICO DIED BECAUSE HIS
IDEAS WERE CRAZY AND TOO
CONTAGIOUS. FRIDAY, SOME
RAPIST DIED BECAUSE HE LEFT HIS
VICTIM WISHING SHE WAS DEAD.
HE HAD TO DIE WISHING HE WAS
ALIVE. SATURDAY, I KILLED A
CONDEMNED MAN SO NO ONE
ELSE WOULD GET BLOOD ON HIS
HANDS. SUNDAY, I RESTED. MONDAY,
SIX PEOPLE JUMPED ME SO I CUT
THEM WITHOUT THINKING.

PEOPLE MUST PAY FOR WHAT THEY
HOLD, FOR WHAT THEY STEAL. YOU
HAVE LIVED OFF THE FAT OF THE
LAND. NOW YOU ARE THE PIG WHO
IS READY FOR SLAUGHTER. YOU ARE
THE OLD ENEMY, THE NEW VICTIM.
WHEN YOU DO SOMETHING AWFUL
EXPECT RETRIBUTION IN KIND.
LOOK OVER YOUR SHOULDER.
SOMEONE IS FOLLOWING. THE POOR
YOU HAVE ROBBED AND IGNORED
ARE IMPATIENT. PLEAD INNOCENT;
YOUR SQUEALS INVITE TORTURE.
PROMISE TO BE GOOD; YOUR LIES
EXCITE AND INFLAME. YOU ARE
TOO DEPRAVED TO REFORM, TOO
TREACHEROUS TO SPARE, TOO
HIDEOUS FOR MERCY. RUN! JUMP!
HIDE! PROVIDE SPORT FOR THE
HUNTERS.

REJOICE! OUR TIMES ARE INTOLERABLE. TAKE COURAGE, FOR THE WORST IS A HARBINGER OF THE BEST. ONLY DIRE CIRCUMSTANCE CAN PRECIPITATE THE OVERTHROW OF OPPRESSORS. THE OLD AND CORRUPT MUST BE LAID TO WASTE BEFORE THE JUST CAN TRIUMPH. OPPOSITION IDENTIFIES AND ISOLATES THE ENEMY. CONFLICT OF INTEREST MUST BE SEEN FOR WHAT IT IS. DO NOT SUPPORT PALLIATIVE GESTURES; THEY CONFUSE THE PEOPLE AND DELAY THE INEVITABLE CONFRONTATION. DELAY IS NOT TOLERATED FOR IT JEOPARDIZES THE WELL-BEING OF THE MAJORITY. CONTRADICTION WILL BE HEIGHTENED, THE RECKONING WILL BE HASTENED BY THE STAGING OF SEED DISTURBANCES. THE APOCALYPSE WILL BLOSSOM.

SENTIMENTALITY DELAYS THE REMOVAL OF THE POLITICALLY BACKWARD AND THE ORGANICALLY UNSOUND. RIGOROUS SELECTION IS MANDATORY IN SOCIAL AND GENETIC ENGINEERING. INCORRECT MERCIFUL IMPULSES POSTPONE THE CLEANSING THAT PRECEDES REFORM. SHORT-TERM NICETIES MUST YIELD TO LONG-RANGE NECESSITY. MORALS WILL BE REVISED TO MEET THE REQUIREMENTS OF TODAY. MEANINGLESS PLATITUDES WILL BE PULLED FROM TONGUES AND MINDS. WORDS LIKE "PURGE" AND "EUTHANASIA" DESERVE NEW CONNOTATIONS. THEY SHOULD BE RECOGNIZED AS THE RATIONAL PUBLIC POLICIES THEY ARE. THE GREATEST DANGER IS NOT EXCESSIVE ZEAL BUT UNDUE HESITATION. WE WILL LEARN TO IMITATE NATURE. HER KILLS NOURISH STRONG LIFE. SQUEAMISHNESS IS THE CRIME.

REPRESSING SEX URGES IS SO BAD. POISON DAMS UP INSIDE AND THEN IT MUST COME OUT. WHEN SEX IS HELD BACK TOO LONG IT COMES OUT FAST AND WILD. IT CAN DO A LOT OF HARM. INNOCENT PEOPLE GET SHOT OR CUT BY CONFUSED SEX URGES. THEY DON'T KNOW WHAT HIT THEM UNTIL TOO LATE. PARENTS SHOULD LET CHILDREN EXPRESS THEMSELVES SO THEY DON'T GET MEAN EARLY. ADULTS SHOULD MAKE SURE THEY FIND MANY OUTLETS. ALL PEOPLE SHOULD RESPOND TO BIG SEX NEEDS. DON'T MAKE FUN OF INDIVIDUALS AND SEND THEM AWAY. IT'S BETTER TO VOLUNTEER THAN TO GET FORCED.

SHRIEK WHEN THE PAIN HITS DURING INTERROGATION. REACH INTO THE DARK AGES TO FIND A SOUND THAT IS LIQUID HORROR, A SOUND OF THE BRINK WHERE MAN STOPS AND THE BEAST AND NAMELESS CRUEL FORCES BEGIN. SCREAM WHEN YOUR LIFE IS THREATENED. FORM A NOISE SO TRUE THAT YOUR TORMENTOR RECOGNIZES IT AS A VOICE THAT LIVES IN HIS OWN THROAT. THE TRUE SOUND TELLS HIM THAT HE CUTS HIS FLESH WHEN HE CUTS YOURS, THAT HE CANNOT THRIVE AFTER HE TORTURES YOU. SCREAM THAT HE DESTROYS ALL THE KINDNESS IN YOU AND BLACKENS EVERY VISION YOU COULD HAVE SHOWN HIM.

RUIN YOUR FUCKING SELF BEFORE THEY DO. OTHERWISE THEY'LL SCREW YOU BECAUSE YOU'RE A NOBODY. THEY'LL KEEP YOU ALIVE BUT YOU'LL HAVE TO CRAWL AND SAY "THANK YOU" FOR EVERY BONE THEY THROW. YOU MIGHT AS WELL STAY DRUNK OR SHOOT JUNK AND BE A CRAZY FUCKER. IF THE RICH GUYS WANT TO PLAY WITH YOU, MAKE THEM GET THEIR HANDS DIRTY. SEND THEM AWAY GAGGING, OR SOBBING IF THEY'RE SOFTHEARTED. YOU'LL BE LEFT ALONE IF YOU'RE FRIGHTENING, AND DEAD YOU'RE FREE! YOU CAN CHANGE THE RADIANT CHILD IN YOU TO A REFLECTION OF THE SHIT YOU WERE MEANT TO SERVE.

SNAKES ARE EVIL INCARNATE. THEY ARE A MANIFESTATION OF THE DARK SIDE OF NATURE. THEY LIE TWINED IN DAMP PLACES, THEIR BODIES COLD TO THE TOUCH. THE FORM OF THE SNAKE IS DREADFUL; THE TONGUE AND WORM-BODY INSPIRE LOATHING. THE SERPENT IS SLY, HE ABIDES WHERE YOU KNOW NOT. HE COMES CRAWLING TO BITE AND POISON. HE HAS MULTIPLIED SO HE INFESTS THE FACE OF THE EARTH. HE IS NOT CONTENT TO BE, HE MUST CORRUPT THAT WHICH IS PURE. THE APPEARANCE OF THE SERPENT SIGNIFIES THAT ALL IS LOST. HE IS A SYMBOL OF OUR FAILURE AND OUR FATE.

opposite: From *Inflammatory Essays*. Offset print on paper with graffiti, 17 x 17 inches each. Street installation, Seattle, Washington, 1984. Organized by Seattle Art Museum.

THE END OF THE U.S.A.
ALL YOU RICH FUCKERS SEE THE
BEGINNING OF THE END AND
TAKE WHAT YOU CAN WHILE
YOU CAN. YOU IMAGINE THAT
YOU WILL GET AWAY, BUT
YOU'VE SHIT IN YOUR OWN BED
AND YOU'RE THE ONE TO SLEEP
IN IT. WHY SHOULD EVERYONE
ELSE STAY BEHIND AND SMELL
YOUR STINKING COWARDICE?
HERE'S A MESSAGE TO YOU—
SPACE TRAVEL IS UNCERTAIN
AND ANY REFUGE OF YOURS
CAN BE BLOWN OFF THE MAP.
THERE'S NO OTHER PLACE FOR
YOU TO GO. KNOW THAT YOUR
FUTURE IS WITH US SO DON'T
GIVE US MORE REASONS TO
HATE YOU.

THE MOST EXQUISITE PLEASURE IS
DOMINATION. NOTHING CAN
COMPARE WITH THE FEELING. THE
MENTAL SENSATIONS ARE EVEN
BETTER THAN THE PHYSICAL ONES.
KNOWING YOU HAVE POWER HAS
TO BE THE BIGGEST HIGH, THE
GREATEST COMFORT. IT IS
COMPLETE SECURITY, PROTECTION
FROM HURT. WHEN YOU DOMINATE
SOMEBODY YOU'RE DOING HIM A
FAVOR. HE PRAYS SOMEONE WILL
CONTROL HIM. YOU'RE HELPING
HIM WHILE HELPING YOURSELF.
EVEN WHEN YOU GET MEAN HE
LIKES IT. SOMETIMES HE'S ANGRY
AND FIGHTS BACK BUT YOU CAN
HANDLE IT. HE ALWAYS REMEMBERS
WHAT HE NEEDS. YOU ALWAYS GET
WHAT YOU WANT.

WHAT SCARES PEASANTS IS
THINKING THEIR BODIES WILL BE
THROWN OUT IN PUBLIC AND LEFT
TO ROT. THEY FEEL SHAME—AS IF
IT MATTERS WHAT POSITION THEIR
LEGS ARE IN WHEN THEY'RE DEAD.
LUCKY THEY'RE SUPERSTITIOUS
BECAUSE THEY'RE EASIER TO
MANAGE. MAKE AN EXAMPLE OF
TWO OR THREE REBELS, DROP
THEIR BODIES BY A ROAD, GET
THEM FLAT AND DRY SO BONES
SHOW AND THE GRASS WEARS
THE CLOTHES. SHOOT THE FINGERS
OFF ANYONE WHO COMES TO
COLLECT THE REMAINS. THOSE BODIES
STAY AS A SIGN OF ABSOLUTE
AUTHORITY. IF PEASANTS THINK
THAT THEIR SOULS CAN'T REST, SO
MUCH THE BETTER.

WHEN YOU START TO LIKE PAIN THINGS
GET INTERESTING. PAIN IS THE COMMON
RESULT OF A SUBORDINATE POSITION.
TRADITIONALLY, SUFFERING IS
UNCOMFORTABLE AND UNDESIRABLE.
PERHAPS IT IS MORE INTELLIGENT TO
CULTIVATE PAIN AS A MEANS OF
LIBERATION? IS IT POSSIBLE THAT
ENJOYMENT OF PAIN CAN BE
SUBVERSIVE? WHEN ONE DOES NOT
FEAR PAIN, ONE CANNOT BE
MANIPULATED. WHEN AROUSED BY
SUFFERING, ONE CAN CONTROL ANY
RELATIONSHIP. WHEN AGONY CEASES
TO BE A BARRIER, DEATH IS NOT
FORBIDDING. THE IMPLICATIONS ARE
MARVELOUS. PAIN IS NOT OPPRESSIVE,
BUT STRENGTHENING AND MOST
SUBLIME. IT IS NECESSARY ONLY TO
DENY THE PLEASURE-PAIN DICHOTOMY.

YOU GET AMAZING SENSATIONS FROM
GUNS. YOU GET RESULTS FROM GUNS.
MAN IS AN AGGRESSIVE ANIMAL; YOU
HAVE TO HAVE A GOOD OFFENSE AND
A GOOD DEFENSE. TOO MANY
CITIZENS THINK THEY ARE HELPLESS.
THEY LEAVE EVERYTHING TO THE
AUTHORITIES AND THIS CAUSES
CORRUPTION. RESPONSIBILITY SHOULD
GO BACK WHERE IT BELONGS. IT IS
YOUR LIFE SO TAKE CONTROL AND
FEEL VITAL. THERE MAY BE SOME
ACCIDENTS ALONG THE PATH TO
SELF-EXPRESSION AND SELF-
DETERMINATION. SOME HARMLESS
PEOPLE WILL BE HURT. HOWEVER,
G-U-N SPELLS PRIDE TO THE STRONG,
SAFETY TO THE WEAK AND HOPE TO
THE HOPELESS. GUNS MAKE WRONG
RIGHT FAST.

YOU GET SO YOU DON'T EVEN
NOTICE THE HALF-DEAD
VAGRANTS ON THE STREET.
THEY'RE ONLY DIRTY GHOSTS.
THE ONES WHO SEND SHIVERS
DOWN YOUR SPINE ARE THE
UNEMPLOYED WHO AREN'T WEAK
YET. THEY STILL CAN FIGHT AND
RUN WHEN THEY WANT TO. THEY
STILL THINK, AND THEY KNOW
THEY HATE YOU. YOU WON'T BE
A PRETTY SIGHT IF THEY GO FOR
YOU. WHEN YOU'RE OUT
WALKING YOU LOOK AT THE MEN
FOR SIGNS OF LINGERING HEALTH
AND OBVIOUS HATRED. YOU
EVEN WATCH THE FALLEN ONES
WHO MIGHT MAKE A LAST MOVE,
WHO MIGHT CLAW YOUR ANKLE
AND TAKE YOU DOWN.

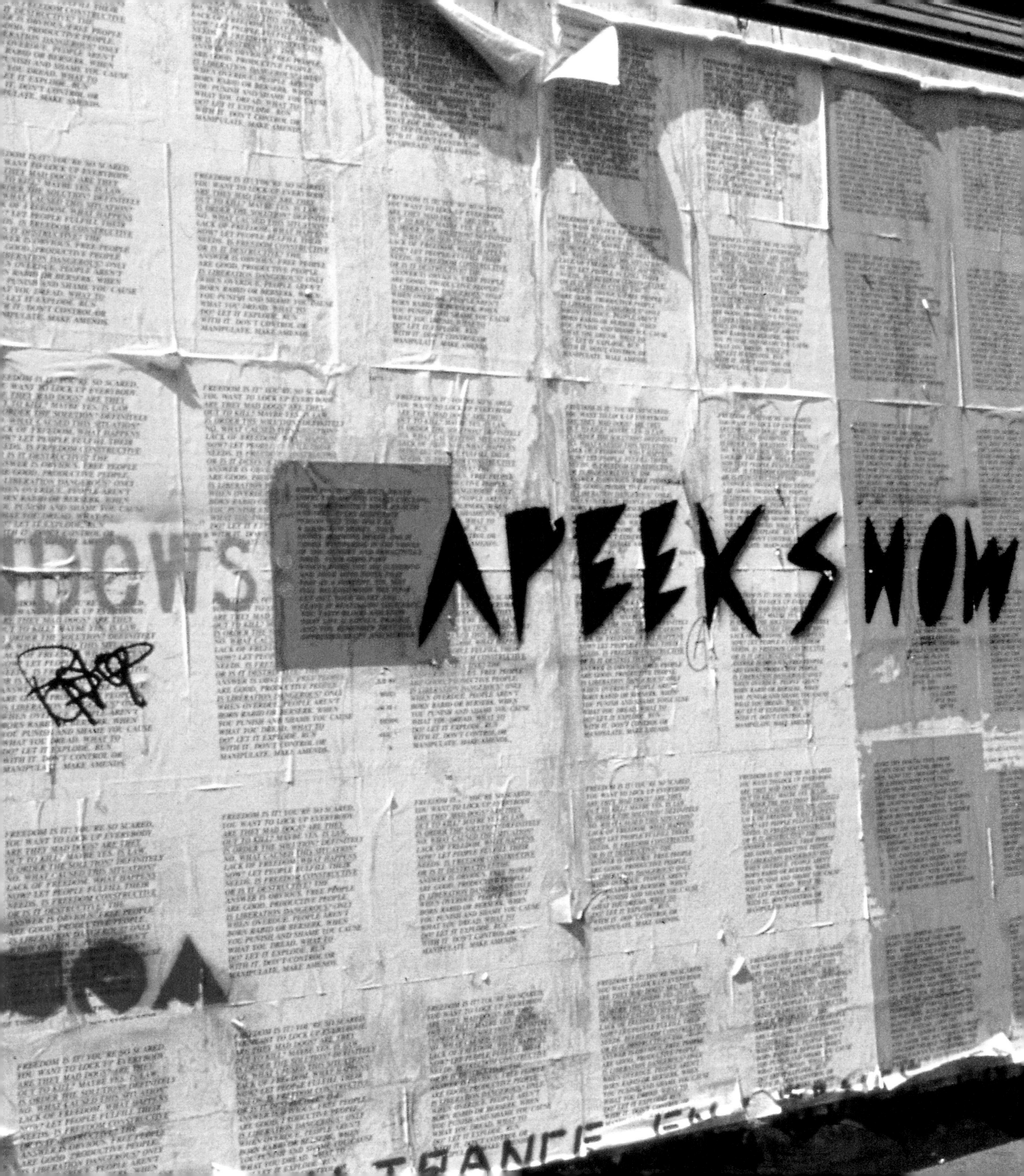
APEEK SHOW

REPRESSING SEX URGES IS SO BAD. POISON DAMS UP INSIDE AND THEN IT MUST COME OUT. WHEN SEX IS HELD BACK TOO LONG IT COMES OUT FAST AND WILD. IT CAN DO A LOT OF HARM. INNOCENT PEOPLE GET SHOT OR CUT BY CONFUSED SEX URGES. THEY DON'T KNOW WHAT HIT THEM UNTIL TOO LATE. PARENTS SHOULD LET CHILDREN EXPRESS THEMSELVES SO THEY DON'T GET TOO WILD AS ADULTS. ADULTS SHOULD MAKE SURE THEY FIND MANY OUTLETS. ALL PEOPLE SHOULD REALIZE BIG SEX NEEDS. DON'T MAKE SIN OF INDIVIDUALS AND SEND THEM AWAY. IT'S BETTER TO VOLUNTEER THAN TO GET FORCED.

From *Inflammatory Essays*. Offset print on paper with graffiti, 10 x 10 inches. Street installation, New York, 1982.

opposite: From *Truisms* and *Inflammatory Essays*. Offset print on paper; 34¾ x 23⅞ inches (*Truisms*), 17 x 17 inches (*Inflammatory Essays*) each. Street installation, Seattle, Washington, 1984. Organized by Seattle Art Museum.

IT'S NICE WHEN YOU DECIDE YOU LIKE SOMEONE AND, WITHOUT DECLARING YOURSELF, DO WHAT'S POSSIBLE TO FURTHER HIS HAPPINESS. THIS CAN TAKE THE FORM OF GIFTS, LOVELY FOOD, PUBLICITY, OR ADVANCE WARNING.

SOMETIMES YOU HAVE NO OTHER CHOICE BUT TO WATCH SOMETHING GRUESOME OCCUR. YOU DON'T HAVE THE OPTION OF CLOSING YOUR EYES BECAUSE IT HAPPENS FAST AND ENTERS YOUR MEMORY.

THE SMALLEST THING CAN MAKE SOMEBODY SEXUALLY UNAPPEALING. A MISPLACED MOLE OR A PARTICULAR HAIR PATTERN CAN DO IT. THERE'S NO REASON FOR THIS BUT IT'S JUST AS WELL.

YOU CAN WATCH PEOPLE ALIGN THEMSELVES WHEN TROUBLE IS IN THE AIR. SOME PREFER TO BE CLOSE TO THOSE AT THE TOP AND OTHERS WANT TO BE CLOSE TO THOSE NEAR THE BOTTOM. IT'S A QUESTION OF WHO FRIGHTENS THEM MORE AND WHOM THEY WANT TO BE LIKE.

IT'S NO FUN WATCHING PEOPLE WOUND THEMSELVES SO THAT THEY CAN HOLE UP, NURSE THEMSELVES BACK TO HEALTH, AND REPEAT THE CYCLE. THEY DON'T KNOW WHAT ELSE TO DO.

HANDS-ON SOCIALIZATION PROMOTES HAPPY INTERPERSONAL RELATIONS. THE DESIRE FOR AND THE DEPENDENCE UPON FONDLING ENSURE REPEATED ATTEMPTS TO OBTAIN CARESSES AND THE WILLINGNESS TO RECIPROCATE.

THE MOUTH IS INTERESTING BECAUSE IT'S ONE OF THOSE PLACES WHERE THE DRY OUTSIDE MOVES TOWARD THE SLIPPERY INSIDE.

THE RICH KNIFING VICTIM CAN FLIP AND FEEL LIKE THE AGGRESSOR IF HE THINKS ABOUT PRIVILEGE. HE ALSO CAN FIND THE CUT SYMBOLIC OR PROPHETIC.

HAVING TWO OR THREE PEOPLE IN LOVE WITH YOU IS LIKE MONEY IN THE BANK.

HOW DO YOU RESIGN YOURSELF TO SOMETHING THAT WILL NEVER BE? YOU STOP WANTING THAT THING, YOU GO NUMB, OR YOU KILL THE AGENT OF DESIRE.

I SAW THEM STRIP A MAN SO THAT IN A MATTER OF SECONDS HE LAY CURLED AND NAKED ON THE SIDEWALK.

IF YOUR CLOTHES CATCH ON FIRE, DROP DOWN IMMEDIATELY, ROLL UP IN A BLANKET, COAT, OR RUG TO SMOTHER THE FLAMES, REMOVE ALL SMOLDERING CLOTHING, AND CALL A DOCTOR OR AMBULANCE.

YOU HAVE TO MAKE THOUSANDS OF PRECISE AND RAPID MOVEMENTS TO PREPARE A MEAL. CHOPPING, STIRRING, AND TURNING PREDOMINATE. AFTERWARDS, YOU STACK AND MAKE CIRCULAR CLEANING AND RINSING MOTIONS. SOME PEOPLE NEVER COOK BECAUSE THEY DON'T LIKE IT, SOME NEVER COOK BECAUSE THEY HAVE NOTHING TO EAT. FOR SOME, COOKING IS A ROUTINE, FOR OTHERS, AN ART.

IF YOU'RE SMART, YOU WATCH FOR CHANGES IN COLOR. THIS CAN APPLY TO SEEING THAT FRUIT IS RIPE OR NOTICING THE FLUSH THAT GOES WITH FEVER, DRUNKENNESS, OR ANGER.

WHEN YOU'RE ON THE VERGE OF DETERMINING THAT YOU DON'T LIKE SOMEONE IT'S AWFUL WHEN HE SMILES AND HIS TEETH LOOK ABSOLUTELY EVEN AND FALSE.

IT CAN BE STARTLING TO SEE SOMEONE'S BREATH, LET ALONE THE BREATHING OF A CROWD. YOU DON'T BELIEVE THAT PEOPLE EXTEND THAT FAR.

IT IS HARD TO KNOW WHAT SOMEONE WANTS BECAUSE YOU CAN'T ACTUALLY FEEL HIS NEEDS. YOU DEVELOP WAYS TO READ OR ANTICIPATE DEMANDS OR YOU WAIT UNTIL YOU'RE ASSAULTED AND THEN HIS REQUIREMENTS BECOME TANGIBLE.

YOU REALIZE THAT YOU'RE ALWAYS SHEDDING PARTS OF THE BODY AND LEAVING MEMENTOS EVERYWHERE.

AFFLUENT COLLEGE-BOUND STUDENTS FACE THE REAL PROSPECT OF DOWNWARD MOBILITY. FEELINGS OF ENTITLEMENT CLASH WITH THE AWARENESS OF IMMINENT SCARCITY. THERE IS RESENTMENT AT GROWING UP AT THE END OF AN ERA OF PLENTY COUPLED WITH REASSESSMENT OF CONVENTIONAL MEASURES OF SUCCESS.

WHEN ONE LEG IS SHORTER THAN THE OTHER YOU KNOW THAT THE BODY WILL WARP AND MANY PARTS WILL TWIST OUT OF ALIGNMENT. YOU CAN HOPE THE ADJUSTMENTS WON'T BE CRIPPLING OR YOU CAN OPERATE TO MAKE THE LEGS THE SAME.

IF SOMEONE IS WILD, PUNISHMENT WILL LEAVE HIM SULLEN AND WILL ONLY MAKE HIM WAIT FOR ANOTHER CHANCE. HE DOESN'T HAVE THE IDEA THAT UNACCEPTABLE BEHAVIOR CAUSES PAIN AND MUST, AT ALL COSTS, BE AVOIDED.

WHEN SOMEONE IS BREATHING ON YOU, YOU FEEL COOL AIR PULLED ACROSS YOUR SKIN FOLLOWED BY MOIST WARM AIR PUSHED IN THE OPPOSITE DIRECTION. THIS OCCURS AT REGULAR INTERVALS AND MAKES A PERFECT TEMPERATURE.

AFTER DARK IT'S A RELIEF TO SEE A GIRL WALKING TOWARD OR BEHIND YOU. THEN YOU'RE MUCH LESS LIKELY TO BE ASSAULTED.

YOU LEARN, THE HARD WAY, TO KEEP A FINGER ON YOUR NIPPLE WHEN SHAVING YOUR BREAST.

YOUR BODY REFUSES TO OBEY WHEN YOU'RE VERY SICK. THE WORST IS WHEN YOU'RE ALERT BUT INCAPABLE OF WILLING YOURSELF ERECT.

IT'S AN ODD FEELING WHEN YOU TRIGGER INSTINCTIVE BEHAVIOR, LIKE NURSING, IN SOMEONE. IT'S FUNNY TO BE IN HIS PRESENCE WHILE A DIFFERENT PART OF THE NERVOUS SYSTEM TAKES OVER AND HIS EYES GET STRANGE.

BY YOUR RESPONSE TO DANGER IT IS EASY TO TELL HOW YOU HAVE LIVED AND WHAT HAS BEEN DONE TO YOU. YOU SHOW WHETHER YOU WANT TO STAY ALIVE, WHETHER YOU THINK YOU DESERVE TO, AND WHETHER YOU BELIEVE IT'S ANY GOOD TO ACT.

EFFIGIES LET YOU STUDY OR ACT UPON SOMEONE WITH IMPUNITY. THEY ARE GOOD FOR PRACTICE.

EVEN WITH YOUR EYES CLOSED YOU CAN SEE SOMEONE APPROACHING. HIS SHADOW SHOWS ON THE INSIDES OF YOUR EYELIDS.

IT'S SCARY WHEN THE VEINS ARE SO CLOSE TO THE SURFACE THAT THEY'RE VISIBLE AND EVEN PROTUBERANT. ACCESS IS EASY TO THE BLOOD THAT TRANSPORTS THE NECESSARY CHEMICALS.

YOU SHOULD LIMIT THE NUMBER OF TIMES YOU ACT AGAINST YOUR NATURE, LIKE SLEEPING WITH PEOPLE YOU HATE. IT'S INTERESTING TO TEST YOUR CAPABILITIES FOR A WHILE BUT TOO MUCH WILL CAUSE DAMAGE.

IT'S AN EXTRAORDINARY FEELING WHEN PARTS OF YOUR BODY ARE TOUCHED FOR THE FIRST TIME. I'M THINKING OF THE SENSATIONS FROM SEX AND SURGERY.

GIFTED CHILDREN, THOSE WITH AN IQ OF 125 OR ABOVE, ARE PRONE TO FEELINGS OF ALIENATION, FRUSTRATION, AND BOREDOM. THESE FEELINGS CAN CULMINATE IN VIOLENCE IF THE CHILDREN ARE NOT ENCOURAGED AND CHALLENGED.

IT MAKES A DIFFERENCE WITH WHOM YOU'RE INTIMATE AND UPON WHOM YOU'RE DEPENDENT. FRIENDS WILL ONLY TOLERATE CERTAIN ACTIONS AND THIS INFLUENCES WHAT YOU BELIEVE TO BE POSSIBLE OR DESIRABLE.

THERE IS A TERRIBLE PHASE WHEN ABUSED ANIMALS OR CHILDREN ACT POLITELY AND TRY TO DO EVERYTHING RIGHT. BY THIS STAGE, THOUGH, THEY ARE SO OBVIOUSLY WEAK AND UNAPPEALING THAT THEY GET LITTLE RESPONSE. IF THEY DON'T DIE THEY BECOME SAVAGE.

IT TAKES A WHILE BEFORE YOU CAN STEP OVER INERT BODIES AND GO AHEAD WITH WHAT YOU WERE TRYING TO DO.

IT'S A SAFE GAME TO PLAY WITH YOUR NOSE, SHUTTING OFF THE AIR AND LETTING IT FLOW AGAIN. THEN YOU CAN ESCALATE AND SEE HOW LONG YOU LAST UNTIL YOU PASS OUT, YOUR HAND RELAXES, AND YOU BREATHE NORMALLY AGAIN.

IT'S EASY FOR YOU TO FEEL BETRAYED WHEN YOU'RE JUST WAVING YOUR ARMS AROUND AND THEY COME CRASHING DOWN ON A SHARP OBJECT.

JUST ONE ROTTEN SPOT IN YOUR HEAD CAN MAKE EVERY MOVEMENT PAINFUL. YOU CAN'T ROLL YOUR EYES, BEND DOWN, OR JUMP AND LAND WITH IMPUNITY. EVEN THINKING HURTS.

LITTLE QUEENIE
ANY NUMBER OF ADOLESCENT GIRLS LIE FACE DOWN ON THE BED AND WORK ON ENERGY, HOUSING, LABOR, JUSTICE, EDUCATION, TRANSPORTATION, AGRICULTURE, AND BALANCE OF TRADE.

MORE PEOPLE WILL BE BUILDING HIDING PLACES IN THEIR HOMES, SMALL REFUGES THAT ARE UNDETECTABLE EXCEPT BY SOPHISTICATED DEVICES.

THERE IS A PERIOD WHEN IT IS CLEAR THAT YOU HAVE GONE WRONG BUT YOU CONTINUE. SOMETIMES THERE IS A LUXURIOUS AMOUNT OF TIME BEFORE ANYTHING BAD HAPPENS.

MORE THAN ONCE I'VE AWAKENED WITH TEARS RUNNING DOWN MY CHEEKS. I HAVE TO THINK WHETHER I WAS CRYING OR WHETHER IT IS INVOLUNTARY, LIKE DROOLING.

PEOPLE LIKE TO BREED ANIMALS. DEVELOPING AND THEN REPLICATING NEW TRAITS IS VERY PLEASING. THE FEAR AND THE ATTRACTION ARE THAT THE PROCESS IS UNCONTROLLABLE.

SOME DAYS YOU WAKE AND IMMEDIATELY START TO WORRY. NOTHING IN PARTICULAR IS WRONG, IT'S JUST THE SUSPICION THAT FORCES ARE ALIGNING QUIETLY AND THERE WILL BE TROUBLE.

SOMEONE WANTS TO CUT A HOLE IN YOU AND FUCK YOU THROUGH IT, BUDDY.

IF THINGS WERE A LITTLE DIFFERENT YOU WOULD DIGEST YOURSELF THROUGH A CUT IN YOUR MOUTH. IT'S A RELIEF TO KNOW THERE ARE PROVISIONS AGAINST THIS.

SOMETHING HAPPENS TO THE VOICES OF PEOPLE WHO LIVE OUTSIDE. THE SOUNDS ARE UNNATURALLY LOW AND HOARSE AS IF THE COLD AND DAMPNESS HAVE ENTERED THE THROAT.

THERE ARE PLACES THAT ARE SCARRED AND THE SKIN IS PULLED AROUND, LIKE THE NAVEL OR THE HEAD OF THE PENIS, THAT LEAVE YOU THINKING THAT THE BODY IS FRAGILE.

IN A PARADISIAC CLIMATE EVERYTHING IS CLEAR AND SIMPLE WHEN YOU ARE PERFORMING BASIC ACTS NECESSARY FOR SURVIVAL.

IT CAN BE HELPFUL TO THINK OF THEM EATING THEIR FAVORITE FOODS AND OCCASIONALLY THROWING UP AND GETTING BITS STUCK IN THEIR NOSES.

THERE'S NO REASON TO SLEEP CURLED AND BENT. IT'S NOT COMFORTABLE, IT'S NOT GOOD FOR YOU, AND IT DOESN'T PROTECT YOU FROM DANGER. IF YOU'RE WORRIED ABOUT AN ATTACK YOU SHOULD STAY AWAKE OR SLEEP LIGHTLY WITH LIMBS UNFURLED FOR ACTION.

THERE'S THE SENSATION OF A LOT OF FLESH WHEN EVERY SINGLE HAIR STANDS UP. THIS HAPPENS WHEN YOU ARE COLD AND NAKED, AROUSED, OR SIMPLY TERRIFIED.

TUNNELING IS GOOD FOR TRANSPORTATION, CLANDESTINE MOVEMENT, AND THE DUAL PROSPECT OF SAFETY AND SUFFOCATION.

USUALLY YOU COME AWAY WITH STUFF ON YOU WHEN YOU'VE BEEN IN THEIR THOUGHTS OR BODIES.

WHAT A SHOCK WHEN THEY TELL YOU IT WON'T HURT AND YOU ALMOST TURN INSIDE OUT WHEN THEY BEGIN.

WHEN YOU'VE BEEN SOMEPLACE FOR A WHILE YOU ACQUIRE THE ABILITY TO BE PRACTICALLY INVISIBLE. THIS LETS YOU OPERATE WITH A MINIMUM OF INTERFERENCE.

WITH BLEEDING INSIDE THE HEAD THERE IS A METALLIC TASTE AT THE BACK OF THE THROAT.

IF YOU WERE A GOOD CHILD WITH FAIR PARENTS, YOU WOULD FREEZE IN YOUR TRACKS, GO LIMP, AND TAKE A DESERVED BEATING. A HOLDOVER FROM THIS MIGHT HAVE YOU SUBMIT TO REAL DANGER, BELIEVING THAT SOMEONE IS APPORTIONING JUST PUNISHMENT AND THINKING THEY WILL STOP SHORT OF KILLING YOU.

WITHOUT WARNING YOUNG ADULTS CAN HEMORRHAGE AND DIE. ANEURYSMS—WEAK BALLOON-LIKE SECTIONS OF ARTERIES—ARE THE CAUSE. IF THE BALLOON BREAKS, UNCONTROLLABLE BLEEDING OCCURS. A PARTICULARLY DANGEROUS ANEURYSM IS FOUND IN THE HEAD.

YOU CAN MAKE YOURSELF ENTER SOMEWHERE FRIGHTENING IF YOU BELIEVE YOU'LL PROFIT FROM IT. THE NATURAL RESPONSE IS TO FLEE BUT YOU DON'T ACT THAT WAY ANYMORE.

IF YOU WISH TO LIVE ANONYMOUSLY, SUCCESS IS CONTINGENT ON FORGOING THE MANY BENEFITS ATTACHED TO IDENTIFICATION, AND YOU MUST NEVER BE SCRUTINIZED OR CAPTURED.

EXERCISE BREAKS AT STRATEGIC POINTS DURING THE DAY ENHANCE PRODUCTIVITY AND PROVIDE SIMULTANEOUS SENSATIONS OF RELIEF AND REJUVENATION.

From the *Living* series.
Bethel White granite
benches, 17 x 36 x
18 inches each. Installation,
Solomon R. Guggenheim
Museum, New York,
1989–90.

opposite: From the *Living*
series. Bethel White granite
benches; 17 x 36 x
18 inches each; 50 x
50 feet overall. Permanent
installation, Walker Art
Center, Minneapolis, 1993.

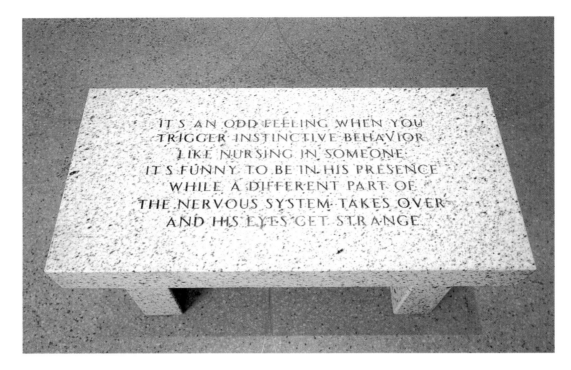

IT'S AN ODD FEELING WHEN YOU
TRIGGER INSTINCTIVE BEHAVIOR
LIKE NURSING IN SOMEONE
IT'S FUNNY TO BE IN HIS PRESENCE
WHILE A DIFFERENT PART OF
THE NERVOUS SYSTEM TAKES OVER
AND HIS EYES GET STRANGE

THERE IS A PERIOD WHEN IT IS CLEAR
THAT YOU HAVE GONE WRONG
BUT YOU CONTINUE
SOMETIMES THERE IS A
LUXURIOUS AMOUNT OF TIME
BEFORE ANYTHING BAD HAPPENS

From the *Living* series.
Hand-painted enamel sign,
21 x 23 inches. 1980.

opposite: From the
Living series. Cast-bronze
plaque, 8 ⅛ x 10 ¼ inches.
Installation, 41 West
Fifty-seventh Street,
New York, 1982.

THE SMALLEST THING CAN MAKE
SOMEONE SEXUALLY UNAPPEALING.
A MISPLACED MOLE OR A PARTICULAR
HAIR PATTERN CAN DO IT. THERE'S
NO REASON FOR THIS, BUT IT'S
JUST AS WELL.

ON HOOD
ERY
LOOR

SANCE
MEDICINE
LOOR

HYSICAL
STUDIO
LOOR

GALLERY
LOOR

S REALTY
RATION
LOOR

MORE THAN ONCE I'VE
WAKENED WITH TEARS
RUNNING DOWN MY CHEEKS.
I HAVE HAD TO THINK
WHETHER I WAS CRYING
OR WHETHER IT WAS
INVOLUNTARY LIKE DROOLING.

opposite: From the *Survival* series (in Polish). Billboard, approximately 13 x 16 feet. Installation, Palace of Culture, Warsaw, 1993. Organized by Center for Contemporary Art, Ujazdowski Castle, Warsaw.

YOU ARE TRAPPED ON THE EARTH SO YOU WILL EXPLODE.

WHAT URGE WILL SAVE US NOW THAT SEX WON'T?

PUT FOOD OUT IN THE SAME PLACE EVERY DAY AND TALK TO THE PEOPLE WHO COME TO EAT AND ORGANIZE THEM.

SAVOR KINDNESS BECAUSE CRUELTY IS ALWAYS POSSIBLE LATER.

DANCE ON DOWN TO THE GOVERNMENT AND TELL THEM YOU'RE EAGER TO RULE BECAUSE YOU KNOW WHAT'S GOOD FOR YOU.

THE BREAKDOWN COMES WHEN YOU STOP CONTROLLING YOURSELF AND WANT THE RELEASE OF A BLOODBATH.

SPIT ALL OVER SOMEONE WITH A MOUTHFUL OF MILK IF YOU WANT TO FIND OUT SOMETHING ABOUT HIS PERSONALITY FAST.

MOTHERS WITH REASONS TO SOB SHOULD DO IT IN GROUPS IN PUBLIC AND WAIT FOR OFFERS.

OUTER SPACE IS WHERE YOU DISCOVER WONDER, WHERE YOU FIGHT AND NEVER HURT EARTH. IF YOU STOP BELIEVING THIS, YOUR MOOD TURNS UGLY.

DIE FAST AND QUIET WHEN THEY INTERROGATE YOU OR LIVE SO LONG THAT THEY ARE ASHAMED TO HURT YOU ANYMORE.

TRUST VISIONS THAT DON'T FEATURE BUCKETS OF BLOOD.

IN A DREAM YOU SAW A WAY TO SURVIVE AND YOU WERE FULL OF JOY.

IF YOU'RE CONSIDERED USELESS NO ONE WILL FEED YOU ANYMORE.

WHEN YOU EXPECT FAIR PLAY YOU CREATE AN INFECTIOUS BUBBLE OF MADNESS AROUND YOU.

YOU ARE SO COMPLEX THAT YOU DON'T ALWAYS RESPOND TO DANGER.

MEN DON'T PROTECT YOU ANYMORE.

WITH ALL THE HOLES IN YOU ALREADY THERE'S NO REASON TO DEFINE THE OUTSIDE ENVIRONMENT AS ALIEN.

WHEN SOMEONE BEATS YOU WITH A FLASHLIGHT YOU MAKE LIGHT SHINE IN ALL DIRECTIONS.

FINDING EXTREME PLEASURE WILL MAKE YOU A BETTER PERSON IF YOU'RE CAREFUL ABOUT WHAT THRILLS YOU.

USE A STUN GUN WHEN THE PERSON COMING AT YOU HAS A GOOD EXCUSE.

IT IS IN YOUR SELF-INTEREST TO FIND A WAY TO BE VERY TENDER.

THE BEGINNING OF THE WAR WILL BE SECRET.

THE CONVERSATION ALWAYS TURNS TO LIVING LONG ENOUGH TO HAVE FUN.

WHAT COUNTRY SHOULD YOU ADOPT IF YOU HATE POOR PEOPLE?

USE WHAT IS DOMINANT IN A CULTURE TO CHANGE IT QUICKLY.

PROTECT ME FROM WHAT I WANT.

YOU ARE CAUGHT THINKING ABOUT KILLING ANYONE YOU WANT.

IT'S HARD TO KNOW IF YOU'RE CRAZY IF YOU FEEL YOU'RE IN DANGER ALL THE TIME NOW.

YOU CAN'T REACH THE PEOPLE WHO CAN KILL YOU ANY TIME SO YOU HAVE TO GO HOME AND THINK ABOUT WHAT TO DO.

THE FUTURE IS STUPID.

HIDE UNDERWATER OR ANYWHERE SO UNDISTURBED YOU FEEL THE JERK OF PLEASURE WHEN AN IDEA COMES.

SOMEONE ELSE'S BODY IS A PLACE FOR YOUR MIND TO GO.

WHEN THERE IS NO SAFE PLACE TO SLEEP YOU'RE TIRED FROM WALKING ALL DAY AND EXHAUSTED FROM THE NIGHT BECAUSE IT'S TWICE AS DANGEROUS THEN.

IT'S EASY TO GET MILLIONS OF PEOPLE ON EVERY CONTINENT TO PLEDGE ALLEGIANCE TO EATING AND EQUAL OPPORTUNITY.

GO WHERE PEOPLE SLEEP AND SEE IF THEY'RE SAFE.

HANDS ON YOUR BREAST CAN KEEP YOUR HEART BEATING.

TURN SOFT AND LOVELY ANY TIME YOU HAVE A CHANCE.

IT IS FUN TO WALK CARELESSLY IN A DEATH ZONE.

YOU LIVE THE SURPRISE RESULTS OF OLD PLANS.

LET YOUR HAND WANDER ON FLESH TO MAKE POSSIBILITY MULTIPLY.

IT IS EMBARRASSING TO BE CAUGHT AND KILLED FOR STUPID REASONS.

SHOOT INTO INFINITE SPACE TO HIT A TARGET IN TIME AND CALL IT
INEVITABLE.

YOU HOVER NEAR LOVELY UNCONSCIOUS LIFE FORMS THAT OFFER NO
IMMEDIATE RESISTANCE.

PEOPLE LOOK LIKE THEY ARE DANCING BEFORE THEY LOVE.

BODIES LIE IN THE BRIGHT GRASS AND SOME ARE MURDERED AND SOME
ARE PICNICKING.

SILLY HOLES IN PEOPLE ARE FOR BREEDING OR FROM SHOOTING.

YOUR MODERN FACE SCANS THE SURPRISE ENDING.

opposite: From the *Survival*
series. Offset print on silver
sticker, 2 ½ x 3 inches.
Street installation, garbage
can lid, New York, 1983.

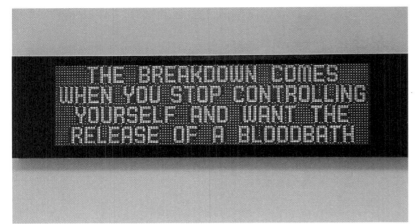

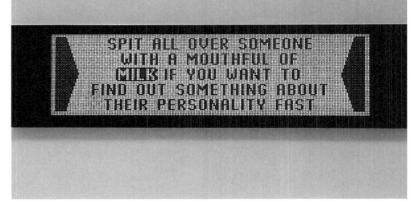

above and opposite:
From the *Survival* series.
UNEX electronic sign,
30 ½ inches x
9 feet 5 ½ inches x
12 inches. Installation,
Barbara Gladstone
Gallery, New York, 1983.

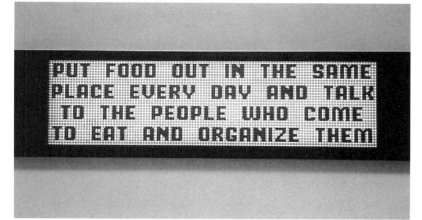

following page: From the *Survival* series. Spectacolor electronic sign, 20 x 40 feet. Installation, Times Square, New York, 1986.

page 85: From the *Survival* series. Electronic sign, 15 x 60 feet. Installation, Showplace Square, San Francisco, 1987. Organized by Artspace, San Francisco.

PROTECT ME FROM WHAT I WANT

SPECTACOLOR 221-8838

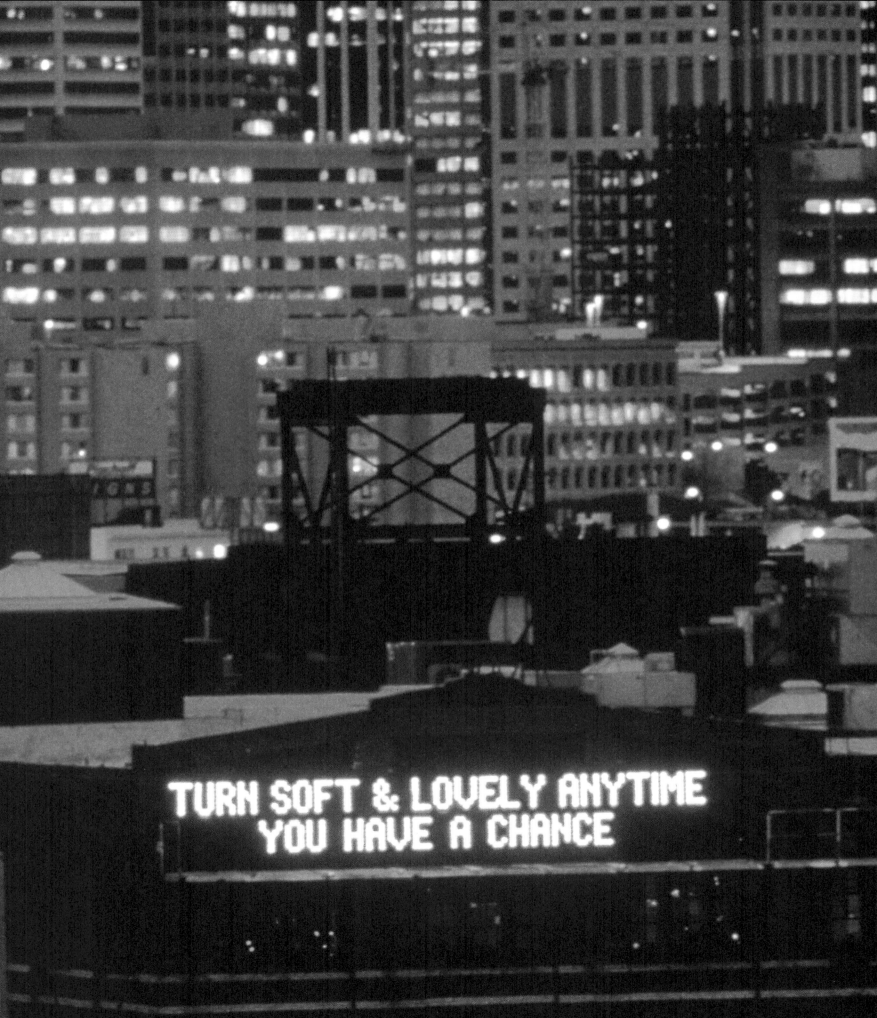

PEOPLE GO TO THE RIVER WHERE IT IS
LUSH AND MUDDY TO SHOOT CAPTIVES,
TO FLOAT OR SINK THEM. SHOTS KILL
MEN WHO ALWAYS WANT. SOMEONE
IMAGINED OR SAW THEM LEAPING TO
SAVAGE THE GOVERNMENT. NOW BODIES
DIVE AND GLIDE IN THE WATER, SCARING
FRIENDS OR MAKING THEM FURIOUS.

UNDER A ROCK, 1986

CRACK THE PELVIS SO SHE LIES RIGHT. THIS IS A MISTAKE. WHEN SHE DIES YOU CANNOT REPEAT THE ACT. THE BONES WILL NOT GROW TOGETHER AGAIN AND THE PERSONALITY WILL NOT COME BACK. SHE IS GOING TO SINK DEEP INTO THE MOSS TO GET WHITE AND LIGHTER. SHE IS UNRESPONSIVE TO BEGGING AND SELF-ABSORBED.

AN OPPOSITION MAN IS CHASED THROUGH HIS TOWN AND SHOT IN A SMELLING TRAP. PEOPLE COME TO POKE LIVE FINGERS THROUGH THE HOLES IN HIM. THEY LOOK AT THEIR FINGERS TO DIVINE WHETHER THEY WILL BE SHOT. THEY SHRINK AND SWELL AND RUN TO HUNT THE PRESIDENT OF THE NATION WHO IS THE TRAPPER.

LIGHT GOES THROUGH BRANCHES TO SHOW TWO CHILDREN BORN AT ONCE WHO MIGHT LIVE. THE MOTHER RAN FROM EVERY HAZARD UNTIL THE BABIES EASED ONTO THE LEAVES. WITH BOTH HANDS SHE BRINGS THEM TO HER MOUTH, CALLING THEM TWICE THE USUAL ANSWER TO MORTAL QUESTIONS. SHE IS DELIGHTFUL AND MILKY SO THEY WILL WANT TO GROW.

BLOOD GOES IN THE TUBE BECAUSE YOU WANT TO FUCK. PUMPING DOES NOT MURDER BUT FEELS LIKE IT. YOU LOSE YOUR WORRYING MIND. YOU WANT TO DIE AND KILL AND WAKE LIKE SILK TO DO IT AGAIN.

PEOPLE GO TO THE RIVER WHERE IT IS LUSH AND MUDDY TO SHOOT CAPTIVES, TO FLOAT OR SINK THEM. SHOTS KILL MEN WHO ALWAYS WANT. SOMEONE IMAGINED OR SAW THEM LEAPING TO SAVAGE THE GOVERNMENT. NOW BODIES DIVE AND GLIDE IN THE WATER, SCARING FRIENDS OR MAKING THEM FURIOUS.

BLOOD KEEPS GOING IN OUTER SPACE UNTIL YOU FORGET. IT STREAMS IN A LINE FROM THE KILLED CONTAINER THAT HAD A MIND. THERE IS NO MATERIAL TO SOAK AND NO MEMORY NEARBY. FRENZY POOLS IN YOU, LOSER, FLYING UPSIDE DOWN. THE CHAMPION GIGGLES THROUGH EVERY POSSIBILITY AND EVOLVES SINGING.

YOU CREATE AN INCIDENT TO BRING THE FURY DOWN. YOUR FIGHTERS BLOW FINGERS AND MORE IN TEN DIRECTIONS. ROUND CROWDS FORM, TRANSFIXED BY THE DEAD. PANIC AND BELATED LOVE TAKE ALL THE SPACE IN BRAINS, AND THE PEOPLE LEFT ALIVE ARE GLAD TO BE FULL. NO ONE EVER KNOWS WHAT TO DO. YOU FIRE AGAIN, AND PEOPLE ARE GRATEFUL ENOUGH.

YOU SPIT ON THEM BECAUSE THE TASTE LEFT ON YOUR TEETH EXCITES. YOU SHOWED HOPE ALL OVER YOUR FACE FOR YEARS AND THEN KILLED THEM IN THE INTEREST OF TIME.

opposite: From *Under a Rock*. Misty Black granite benches and LED sign; benches: 17 ¼ x 48 x 21 inches each; sign: 10 inches x 9 feet 4 ½ inches x 4 ½ inches. Installation, Rhona Hoffman Gallery, Chicago, 1987.

opposite and left: From *Under a Rock*. Sandstone benches, 19¾ x 59¾ x 13¾ inches each. Installation, Schloßgarten Münster, Germany, 1987. Organized by Westfälisches Landesmuseum für Kunst und Kulturgeschichte, Münster.

IF TH
PROCESS ST
I WILL
KILL THIS BA
A GOOD WAY
SHE CAN LIE
ON MY
FAMILIAR BELLY.
OUR BACKS WILL
BE IN LINE
AND THEN
STINGUISHABLE.
ILL TAKE
WN BEFORE
LS THE
AT IS
ND

LAMENTS, 1989

opposite: From *Laments*. Nubian Black granite sarcophagus, 24 ⅜ inches x 6 feet 10 inches x 30 inches. Installation, Williams College Museum of Art, Williamstown, Massachusetts, 1995.

THE NEW DISEASE CAME.
I LEARN THAT TIME
DOES NOT HEAL.
EVERYTHING GETS
WORSE WITH DAYS.
I HAVE SPOTS
LIKE A DOG.
I COUGH AND CANNOT
TURN MY HEAD.
I CONSIDER SLEEPING
WITH PEOPLE
I DO NOT LIKE.
I NEED TO LIE
BACK TO FRONT
WITH SOMEONE
WHO ADORES ME.
I WILL THINK MORE
BEFORE I CANNOT.
I LOVE MY MIND WHEN
IT IS FUCKING THE
CRACKS OF EVENTS.
I WANT TO TELL YOU
WHAT I KNOW
IN CASE IT IS OF USE.
I WANT TO GO TO
THE FUTURE PLEASE.

IF THE
PROCESS STARTS
I WILL
KILL THIS BABY
A GOOD WAY.
SHE CAN LIE
ON MY
FAMILIAR BELLY.
OUR BACKS WILL
BE IN LINE
AND THEN
INDISTINGUISHABLE.
I WILL TAKE
HER DOWN BEFORE
SHE FEELS THE
FEAR THAT IS
CAUSE AND
RESULT.

WITH ONLY MY MIND
TO PROTECT ME
I GO INTO DAYS.
WHAT I FEAR IS
IN A BOX WITH FUR
TO MUFFLE IT.
EVERY DAY I DO NOTHING
BECAUSE I AM
SCARED BLANK AND LAZY,
BUT THEN THE MEN COME.
I PUT MY MOUTH ON THEM.
I SPIT AND WRITE
WITH THE WET.
THE WET SAYS WHAT
MUST STOP AND
WHAT SHALL BEGIN.
I SPIT BECAUSE THE DEATH
SMELL IS TOO CLOSE TO ME.
THE STINK MAKES WORDS
TELL THE TRUTH ABOUT
WHO KILLS AND
WHO IS THE VICTIM.
DEATH IS THE
MODERN ISSUE.

NO RECORD OF JOY
CAN BE LIKE THE
JUICE THAT JUMPS
THROUGH YOUR SKULL
WHEN YOU ARE
PERFECT IN SEX.
YOU POSITION
YOUR SPINE UNTIL
IT WAVES.
YOUR HANDS RUN
TO SPOTS
THAT FEEL
DIFFERENT.
BREATHING TELLS
THE PERSON
WHAT TO DO.
YOU TRY TO STOP
BECAUSE THAT
IS THE FUN.
THEN YOU SQUEEZE
AND BECOME
UNCONSCIOUS NEAR
WHOMEVER WHICH IS
THE DANGEROUS
THING IN
THE WORLD.
AT THE END
YOU DO NOT WANT.
YOU CARRY THIS
SENSATION TO THE
CRUEL PLACES
YOU GO.

THERE IS NO ONE'S
SKIN UNDER
MY FINGERNAILS.
THERE IS NO ONE
TO WATCH
MY HAIR GROW.
NO ONE LOOKS AT
ME WHEN I WALK.
PEOPLE WANT ME
TO PAY MONEY FOR
EACH THING I GET.
I HAVE EVERY KIND
OF THOUGHT AND THAT
IS NO EMBARRASSMENT.
I LOOK AT MYSELF
WHEN I BATHE.
WHAT I GIVE
TO ALL THE PEOPLE
WHO DO NOT WANT
TO LIVE WITH ME
IS ARITHMETIC.
I COUNT INFANTS AND
PREDICT THEIR DAYS.
I SUBTRACT PEOPLE
KILLED FOR ONE
REASON OR ANOTHER.
I GUESS THE NEW
REASONS AND PROJECT
THEIR EFFICACY.
I DECORATE MY
NUMBERS AND
CIRCULATE THEM.

I HAVE A
HOT HOLE
THAT WAS
PUT IN ME.
I CAN LIVE
WITH IT.
PEOPLE MADE IT
AND USE IT
TO GET
TO ME.
I CAN HURT
IT TOO BUT
USUALLY I PUT
MY THINKING
THERE FOR
EXCITEMENT.
WHEN MY MIND
IS RIGHT I
CAN SAY WHAT
NO ONE WANTS
TO HEAR.
I BRAG ABOUT
MY INDIFFERENCE,
BUT THE LAST
KIND PART OF
ME RAVES
BECAUSE
I WILL NOT
BE THE ONLY
DEAD ONE.
I KEEP THE
HOLE OPEN.

THE KNIFE CUT
RUNS AS LONG
AS IT WANTS.
IT IS THROUGH
MY STOMACH.
I KEEP LOOKING
AT IT.
I HAVE MORE
COLORS THAN
I WOULD
HAVE THOUGHT.
THE HOLE IS
LARGE ENOUGH
FOR MY HEAD.
THE HOLE WAS
BIG ENOUGH
FOR THEIR HANDS
TO MOVE FREELY.
THEY PUT THEIR
FINGERS IN
BECAUSE THEY
SHOULD NOT AND
BECAUSE THEY
DO NOT GET
THE CHANCE
EVERY DAY.

I WAS
SICK FROM
ACTING NORMAL.
I WATCHED
REPLAYS OF
THE WAR.
WHEN NOTHING
HAPPENED I
CLOSED A ZONE
WHERE I
EXERT CONTROL.
I FORMED A
GOVERNMENT THAT
IS AS WELCOME
AS SEX.
I AM GOOD
TO PEOPLE
UNTIL THEY DO
SOMETHING STUPID.
I STOP THE
HABITUAL MISTAKES
THAT MAKE FATE.
I GIVE PEOPLE
TIME SO THEY
FEEL THEIR LIVES
MOVING OVER
THEIR SKINS.
I WANT A
LARGER ARENA.
I TEASE WITH
THE POSSIBILITY
OF MY
ABSENCE.

I WANT TO LIVE IN
A SILVER WRAPPER.
I WILL SEE
WHOOPING ROCKS FLY.
I WILL ICE ON MY BLACK SIDE
AND STEAM ON THE OTHER
WHEN I FLOAT BY SUNS.
I WANT TO LICK FOOD
FROM THE CEILING.
I AM AFRAID TO STAY
ON THE EARTH.
FATHER HAS CARRIED ME THIS
FAR ONLY TO HAVE ME BURN
AT THE EDGE OF SPACE.
FACTS STAY IN YOUR MIND
UNTIL THEY RUIN IT.
THE TRUTH IS PEOPLE ARE
PUSHED AROUND BY TWO MEN
WHO MOVE ALL THE
BODIES ON EARTH INTO
PATTERNS THAT PLEASE THEM.
THE PATTERNS SPELL
OH NO NO NO
BUT IT DOES NO GOOD
TO WRITE SYMBOLS.
YOU HAVE TO DO THE
RIGHT ACTS WITH YOUR BODY.
I SEE SPACE AND IT
LOOKS LIKE NOTHING AND
I WANT IT AROUND ME.

DEATH CAME AND HE LOOKED
LIKE A RAT WITH CLAWS.
I MADE HIM GO
INTO THE WALL.
I KEEP HIM THERE WITH
THE PRESSURE OF MY MIND.
I HEAR HIM SCRATCHING
AND CLIMBING.
MY THOUGHTS FLY TO THE
WALL TO SEAL THE CRACKS
AND ADD PLASTER
LAYERS FOR STRENGTH.
I KEEP MY BRAIN ON SO I
DO NOT FALL INTO NOTHING
IF HIS CLAWS HURT ME.
I DO NOT WANT TO LEAVE
MY HOUSE AND THE
PEOPLE I LIKE.
I DO NOT WANT TO STOP
KNOWING ALL MY FACTS.
I DO NOT WANT MY BODY TO
TURN INTO SOMETHING ELSE.
WHEN A RAT MAKES YOU
UNCONSCIOUS YOU GO ON
A CONVEYOR BELT AND ARE
DUMPED FROM THE END.
YOU DROP IN SPACE AND
NEVER HIT BOTTOM EVEN
THOUGH YOU NEED TO
AS TIME PASSES.

I CAN MAKE WOMEN'S
BREASTS WEEP. I DREAM
WORDS. MY IDEAS COME
FROM MY SKIN. I WAKE
IN TERROR FROM WHAT
IS IN ME BEFORE
EXPERIENCE. I CONJURE
WHAT HAS NEVER BEEN
TO DAZZLE MYSELF.
I DO NOT WANT TO BE
LEFT TO BE EATEN.
I MOVE IN AN ENVELOPE
OF ALL SMELLS. I HOOT
WHEN MY BRAIN FILLS.

From *Laments*. Nubian Black granite, Verde Antique marble, Ankara Red marble, and Honey onyx sarcophagi, and vertical LED signs; sarcophagi: 24 ³/₈ inches x 6 feet 10 inches x 30 inches (Nubian Black), 18 ¼ x 54 x 24 inches (Verde Antique), 24 ³/₈ inches x 6 feet 10 inches x 30 inches (Ankara Red), 12 x 36 x 18 inches (Honey) each; signs: 10 feet 8 inches x 10 inches x 4 ½ inches each. Installation, Dia Art Foundation, New York, 1989–90.

following two pages: From *Laments*. Nubian Black granite sarcophagi and vertical LED signs; sarcophagi: 24 ³/₈ inches x 6 feet 10 inches x 30 inches each; signs: 10 feet 8 inches x 10 inches x 4 ½ inches each. Installation, Williams College Museum of Art, Williamstown, Massachusetts, 1995.

pages 98–99: From *Laments*. Nubian Black granite sarcophagus, 24 ³/₈ inches x 6 feet 10 inches x 30 inches. Installation, Williams College Museum of Art, Williamstown, Massachusetts, 1995.

THE NEW D...
I LEARN...
DOES N...
EVERYTH...
WORSE W...
I HAVE...
LIKE A...
I COUGH AN...
TURN M...
I CONSIDE...
WITH...
I DO N...
I NEED...
BACK TO...
WITH SO...
WHO AD...
WILL TH...
BEFORE I...
OVE MY...

SEASE CAME.
HAT TIME
OT HEAL.
NG GETS
TH DAYS.
SPOTS
DOG.
D CANNOT
HEAD.
SLEEPING
EOPLE
OT LIKE.
TO LIE
FRONT
MEONE
RES ME.
NK MORE
CANNOT
MIND WH

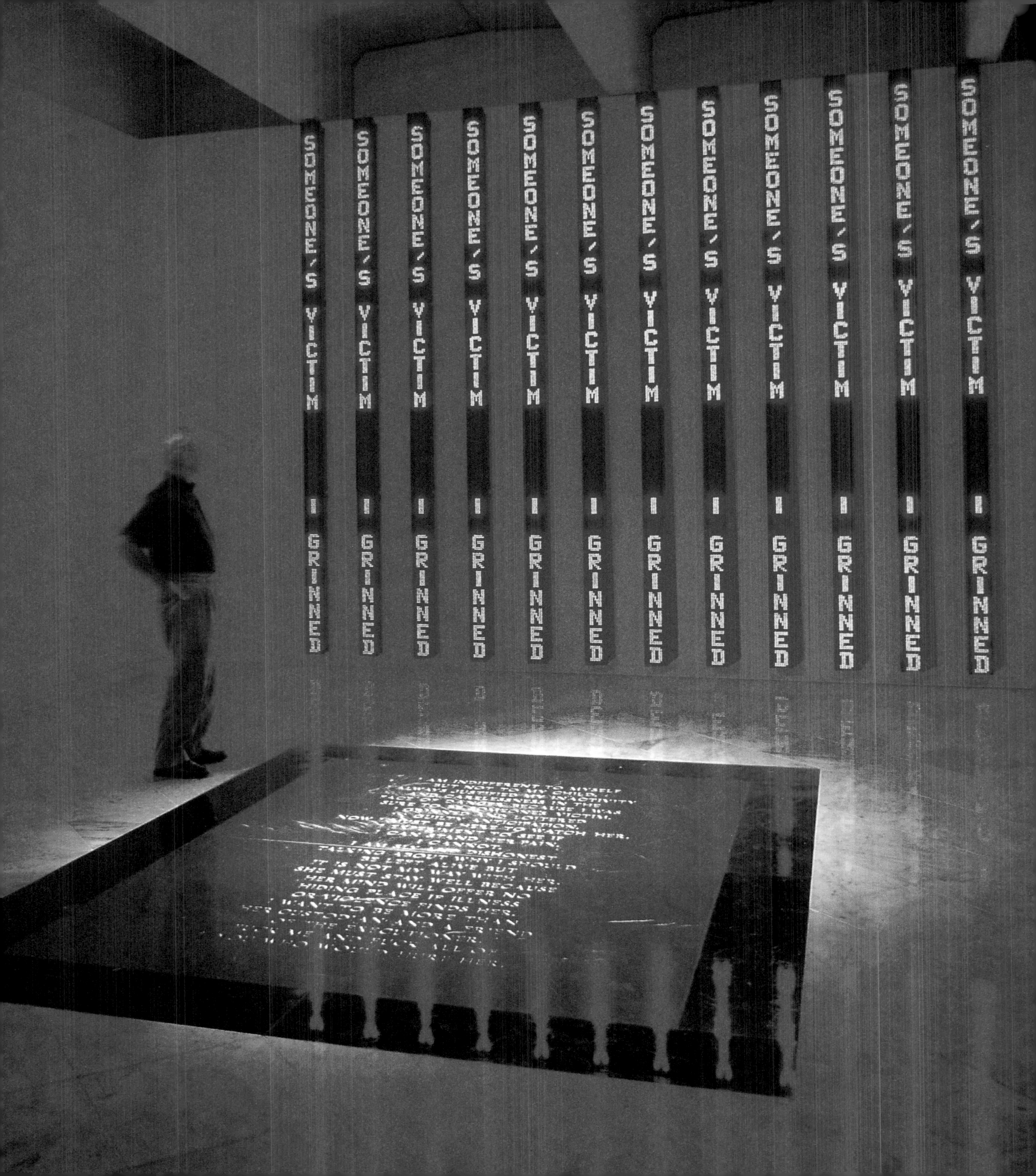
SOMEONE'S VICTIM I GRINNED

MOTHER AND CHILD, 1990

I AM INDIFFERENT TO MYSELF BUT NOT TO MY CHILD. I ALWAYS JUSTIFIED MY INACTIVITY AND CARELESSNESS IN THE FACE OF DANGER BECAUSE I WAS SURE TO BE SOMEONE'S VICTIM. I GRINNED AND LOITERED IN GUILTY ANTICIPATION. NOW I MUST BE HERE TO WATCH HER. I EXPERIMENT TO SEE IF I CAN STAND HER PAIN. I CANNOT. I AM SLY AND DISHONEST TALKING ABOUT WHY I SHOULD BE LEFT ALIVE, BUT IT IS NOT MY WAY WITH HER. SHE MUST STAY WELL BECAUSE HER MIND WILL OFFER NO HIDING PLACE IF ILLNESS OR VIOLENCE FINDS HER. I WANT TO BE MORE THAN HER CUSTODIAN AND A FRIEND OF THE EXECUTIONER. FUCK ME AND FUCK ALL OF YOU WHO WOULD HURT HER.

I DID NOT WANT MY CHILD BECAUSE I KNEW I COULD NOT LIKE THE FEELING WHEN SHE WAS THREATENED, BUT ONE MORNING IN A MOVEMENT OF INFINITE TENDERNESS I CALLED HER. I CANNOT PRECLUDE HER DEATH AND OUR DEPENDENCE LETS EVERY DANGER WORK UNCHALLENGED. THE IDEA THAT I AM CRIMINAL RECURS EACH TIME THERE IS REAL TROUBLE. I WOULD KILL HER RATHER THAN WATCH A DIRTY ENDING BUT THE KILLING WOULD SPOIL MY PITY. IF MY INSTINCT IS RUINED I WILL BE THE PERSON WHO CAN DO ANYTHING TO YOU.

I AM SULLEN AND THEN FRANTIC WHEN I CANNOT BE WHOLLY WITHIN THE ZONE OF MY INFANT. I AM CONSUMED BY HER. I AM AN ANIMAL WHO DOES ALL SHE SHOULD. I AM SURPRISED THAT I CARE WHAT HAPPENS TO HER. I WAS PAST FEELING MUCH BECAUSE I WAS TIRED OF MYSELF BUT I WANT HER TO LIVE. I HATE EACH OF YOU WHO MURDERS. NOW MY BEST SENSES ARE BACK AND WHAT I FEEL AFTER LOVE IS FEAR.

I FEAR FIVE THINGS AND MYSELF.

I FEAR THE NEW ILLNESS. I AM NOT SURE IF THE CHILD AND I ARE SICK. NOW THAT SHE IS BORN I AM AFRAID TO KNOW. I TOUCH HER NECK. I AM NOT CERTAIN I COULD CARE FOR HER.

I FEAR PEOPLE CRAZY MAD FROM NEED AND THE CONTEMPT OF EVERYONE WHO COULD HELP THEM. I GO WALKING AND I HOPE SOMEONE DOES NOT SEE MY FAT BABY AS AN INSULT.

I AM AFRAID OF THE ONES IN POWER WHO KILL PEOPLE AND DO NOT ADMIT GRIEF. THEY WILL NOT STAY IN A ROOM WITH A DYING BABY. THEY WILL NOT SPEND THE DAYS IT CAN TAKE.

I FEAR SUBSTANCES THAT CANNOT BE SENSED AND MUST NOT BE TOUCHED, THE RESIDUE OF GOOD AND BAD IDEAS. I TURN THE CHILD OVER AND OVER TO LOOK FOR SIGNS. CONTAMINATION MAKES THE NEW WEATHER AND THE STINKING HEAT. THE BABY IS RED AND TRIES TO PULL AWAY FROM ME. AFTER THIS IDIOT PERIOD OF SQUANDERING AND WAITING I FEAR EVERYONE WHO DOES NOT WELCOME CHANGE.

THE SHOCK OF A CUTTING BIRTH REMINDS ME THAT PAIN IS NOT THOUGHT. MY NEED TO PROTECT COMES WITH THE CHILD. IT MAY GIVE ME TIME.

opposite: From *Mother and Child*. Ankara Red marble tablet with Nero Marquina marble border and Carrara Goia marble floor tiles, and vertical LED signs; signs: 12 feet 9 ½ inches x 5 ½ inches x 4 inches each. Installation, Walker Art Center, Minneapolis, 1991.

right and opposite:
From *Mother and Child*.
Rosso Magnaboschi
marble tablet with
Nero Marquina marble
border and Biancone
marble floor tiles, and
vertical LED signs; signs:
12 feet 9 ½ inches x
5 ½ inches x 4 inches each.
Installation, Gallery A,
United States Pavilion,
Venice, 1990.

I AM INDIFFERENT TO MYSELF
BUT NOT TO MY CHILD.
I ALWAYS JUSTIFIED MY INACTIVITY
AND CARELESSNESS IN THE
FACE OF DANGER BECAUSE I WAS
SURE TO BE SOMEONE'S VICTIM.
I GRINNED AND LOITERED
IN GUILTY ANTICIPATION.
NOW I MUST BE HERE
TO WATCH HER.
I EXPERIMENT TO SEE IF
I CAN STAND HER PAIN.
I CANNOT.
I AM SLY AND DISHONEST
TALKING ABOUT WHY I SHOULD
BE LEFT ALIVE BUT
IT IS NOT THIS WAY WITH HER.
SHE MUST STAY WELL BECAUSE
HER MIND WILL OFFER NO
HIDING PLACE IF ILLNESS
OR VIOLENCE FINDS HER.
I WANT TO BE MORE THAN
A CUSTODIAN AND A FRIEND
OF THE EXECUTIONER.
FUCK MYSELF AND FUCK ALL OF
YOU WHO WOULD HURT HER.

BURNED ALL OVER SO ONLY HIS TEETH ARE GOOD, HE SITS FUSED TO THE TANK. METAL HOLDS THE BLAST HEAT AND THE SUN. HIS DEATH IS FRESH AND THE SMELL PLEASANT. HE MUST BE PULLED AWAY SKIN SPLITTING. HE IS A SUGGESTION THAT AFFECTS PEOPLE DIFFERENTLY.

THE SHAPE IN THE BLANKET IS STUPID. A TORSO REMAINS. THE MOTHER RECALLS A CHILD'S LOGICAL AND ADEQUATE SHADOW. SHE RUNS HER HAND OVER AND REJECTS THE FLESH.

I GAG ON THE FOOD SHINY WITH OIL AND MUCUS. MY THROAT CLOSES WHEN I TRY TO EAT. THE IRIDESCENCE IS BEAUTIFUL IF I TILT THE PLATE.

I STAB THE BOY. I CUT HOLES TO DRAIN HIM.

HE MOVES LEGLESS AFTER THE HIT. HE IS A PIECE OF SPIDER. HIS ELBOWS MAKE KNEES. HE LEAKS JUICE. HE FLIES NOT DREAMING.

THE OCEAN WASHES THE DEAD. THEY ARE FACE UP FACE DOWN IN FOAM. BODIES ROLL FROM SWELLS TO OPEN IN THE MARSH.

THE ROOTS OF MY TEETH DETECT MOTION AS MY EYES ARE SEWN. MY HAIR CANNOT SEND ANY MORE MESSAGES BUT I HEAR ALL THEIR WORDS.

HIS NECK STRAINS AND PIVOTS. HE BITES IN A CIRCLE AROUND HIM. HE CANNOT RAISE HIS ARMS BECAUSE HE IS PACKED IN MEN. THE THING THAT IS ALL OF THEM BEGINS TO SCREAM.

IT IS THE WAR ZOO. IT IS A LANDMARK. PILOTS NAME IT. THE ANIMAL IS FOLDED IN THE LANDSCAPE. A BONE IS BROKEN SO IT CANNOT MOVE AWAY. INSTINCT MAKES IT WATCHFUL. IT EXPECTS THAT SOMEONE WILL TOUCH IT TO RESTORE THE PACT.

opposite: From *War*. Vertical LED signs, 9 feet 4 ½ inches x 10 inches x 4 ½ inches each. Installation, church of St. Peter, Cologne, 1993.

opposite, left, and following two pages: **BLACK GARDEN.** Black and white planting and Bentheimer Red sandstone benches; benches: 17 ⅜ inches x 6 feet x 24 inches each. Permanent installation, Nordhorn, Germany, 1994. (Left: top, Black Mondo grass; bottom, Queen of the Night tulips.)

opposite: From *Lustmord* (in Japanese). 3-D Imager, 35 x 27 x 27 inches. Installation, Contemporary Art Center, Art Tower Mito, Mito, Japan, 1994.

PERPETRATOR

I SWIM IN HER AS SHE QUIETS.

I SINK ON HER.

I SING HER A SONG ABOUT US.

I STEP ON HER HANDS.

I SPLAY HER FINGERS.

SHE ROOTS WITH HER BLUNT FACE.

SHE HUNTS ME WITH HER MOUTH.

SHE HAS THREE COLORS IN HER EYES.

I BITE HER CLOSED AGAIN.

I AM NEAR HER MILK.

I TELL HER TO SOAP HERSELF.

SHE TIGHTENS AND I HIT HER.

I WASH HER OUT.

I WATCH HER WHILE SHE THINKS ABOUT ME.

HER SALIVA RUNS WHEN SHE SLEEPS.

I HOOK HER SPINE.

SHE HAS A URINE SMELL.

HER SWALLOW REFLEX IS GONE.

HER HEAD EXPLODES IN THE FIRE.

HER BREASTS ARE ALL NIPPLE.

SHE ACTS LIKE AN ANIMAL LEFT FOR COOKING.

I FIND HER SQUATTING ON HER HEELS AND THIS OPENS HER SO I CAN GET HER FROM BELOW.

I TAKE HER FACE WITH ITS FINE HAIRS. I POSITION HER MOUTH.

I WANT TO FUCK HER WHERE SHE HAS TOO MUCH HAIR.

I HOOK MY CHIN OVER HER SHOULDER. NOW THAT SHE IS STILL I CAN CONCENTRATE.

SHE HAS NO TASTE LEFT TO HER AND THIS MAKES IT EASIER FOR ME.

THE COLOR OF HER WHERE SHE IS INSIDE OUT IS ENOUGH TO MAKE ME KILL HER.

VICTIM

I AM AWAKE IN THE PLACE WHERE WOMEN DIE.

THE BIRD TURNS ITS HEAD AND LOOKS WITH ONE EYE WHEN YOU ENTER.

MY BREASTS ARE SO SWOLLEN THAT I BITE THEM.

YOUR AWFUL LANGUAGE IS IN THE AIR BY MY HEAD.

I DO NOT LIKE TO WALK BECAUSE I FEEL IT BETWEEN MY LEGS.

HAIR IS STUCK INSIDE ME.

MY NOSE BROKE IN THE GRASS. MY EYES ARE SORE FROM MOVING AGAINST YOUR PALM.

I HAVE THE BLOOD JELLY.

WITH YOU INSIDE ME COMES THE KNOWLEDGE OF MY DEATH.

YOU HAVE SKIN IN YOUR MOUTH. YOU LICK ME STUPIDLY.

YOU CONFUSE ME WITH SOMETHING THAT IS IN YOU. I WILL NOT PREDICT HOW YOU WANT TO USE ME.

I FEEL YOUR SHOULDER BONE UNDER MY HAND AND I KNOW WHAT WILL COME TO YOU.

I KNOW WHO YOU ARE AND IT DOES ME NO GOOD AT ALL.

I TRY TO EXCITE MYSELF SO I STAY CRAZY.

WHAT IS LEFT ON THE BLANKET IS CLEAR AND THE COLOR OF HELL.

OBSERVER

I WANT TO LIE DOWN BESIDE HER. I HAVE NOT SINCE I WAS A CHILD. I WILL BE COVERED BY WHAT HAS COME FROM HER.

SHE BEGINS TO MAKE MISTAKES IN HER LANGUAGE AND I CORRECT HER THE WAY SHE TAUGHT ME.

I FIND HER TOWELS SHOVED IN TIGHT SPOTS. I TAKE THEM TO BURN ALTHOUGH I FEAR TOUCHING HER THINGS.

SHE SMILES AT ME BECAUSE SHE IMAGINES I CAN HELP HER.

SHE COUGHS THE MOUTH STRINGS.

I WANT TO BRUSH HER HAIR BUT THE SMELL OF HER MAKES ME CROSS THE ROOM. I HELD MY BREATH AS LONG AS I COULD. I KNOW I DISAPPOINT HER.

SHE STARTED RUNNING WHEN EVERYTHING BEGAN POURING FROM HER BECAUSE SHE DID NOT WANT TO BE SEEN.

SHE FELL ON THE FLOOR IN MY ROOM. SHE TRIED TO BE CLEAN WHEN SHE DIED BUT SHE WAS NOT. I SEE HER TRAIL.

HER GORE IS IN A BALL OF CLEANING RAGS. I CARRY OUT THE DAMPNESS LEFT FROM MY MOTHER. I RETURN TO HIDE HER JEWELRY.

THE BLACK SPECKS INSIDE MY EYES FLOAT ON HER BODY. I WATCH THEM WHILE I THINK ABOUT HER.

I WANT TO SUCK ON HER TO MAKE HER RESPOND.

I WALK OUTSIDE TO THE PATH AND SEE THE PLANTS, EACH HANDLED BY HER, UNMARKED BY HER DYING.

SHE IS NARROW AND FLAT IN THE BLUE SACK AND I STAND WHEN THEY LIFT HER.

From *Lustmord*. Offset print (in red ink made from human blood, and in black ink) on paper, attached to cover of *Süddeutsche Zeitung Magazin*, November 19, 1993. With Tibor Kalman. Closed and open views.

opposite and pages 116–17: Photographs of handwriting in ink on skin, 1993. (Reproduced in *Süddeutsche Zeitung Magazin*, November 19, 1993.)

I WANT TO LIE
DOWN BESIDE HER.
I HAVE NOT SINCE
I WAS A CHILD.
I WILL BE COVERED
BY WHAT HAS
COME FROM HER.

I KNOW WHO
YOU ARE AND
IT DOES ME
NO GOOD
AT ALL

I AM
AWAKE IN
THE PLACE
WHERE
WOMEN DIE

right and opposite: *Bone Tables.* Human bones and engraved and etched silver. Installation, Galerie Rähnitzgasse der Landeshauptstadt, Dresden, Germany, 1996.

pages 120–21: *KriegsZustand.* Laser projection. Installation, Völkerschlachtdenkmal Leipzig, Germany, 1996. Organized by Leipziger Galerie für Zeitgenössische Kunst.

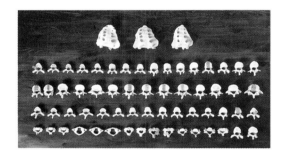

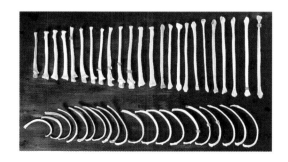

WITH YOU
INSIDE ME
COMES THE
KNOWLEDGE
OF MY DEATH

the color
of her
where she is
inside out is
enough to make
me kill her

KILLING EFFEMINATE
MEN

BITING THE HELPER

PARENTS QUIET WHEN
YOU ARE TAKEN

ALWAYS POLITE TO OFFICERS

SMILING OFTEN TO DISARM

THE ENERGETICALLY CRUEL

BLOOD OUTSIDE FOR ANIMALS

A MEMORY OF DOMINANCE

THE SOLDIER BITES YOUR STOMACH

SNEAKING TO WASH

THE HORSE RUNNING INTO WALLS

NEW TEETH IN THE BABY'S MOUTH

THE BABY MOVES TO YOUR OTHER BREAST

THE FOREARM OF YOUR LOVER

ADDING WATER TO FOOD

FULL OF SWALLOWED BLOOD

SON OF A RAPIST

I RAISE MY ARMS TO HIM

THE CHILD WITH A HAND IN HER

BIRDS EATING THEM

PROPERTY SEIZED BY THE ZEALOUS

YOUR MOTHER WITH NO REAL POWER

THINKING WHILE HELD DOWN

AGREEING TO STAY STILL

WAITING TO BE TRANSPORTED

EYE CUT BY FLYING GLASS

THE CHILD WALKS ON A BROKEN LEG

BONE VISIBLE THROUGH THE FOREHEAD

BITING THE HELPER

CHEWING WOOD FOR COMFORT

DOCILE SO HE IS FAST

DYING FROM KNOWING

PARENTS QUIET WHEN YOU ARE TAKEN

WRITING ON THE WALLS AT NIGHT

KILLING EFFEMINATE MEN

THE BOY URINATES IN CLASS

THE LEGS OF YOUR MOTHER

USING GOD

EXPEDIENT POLICY

NO CHANCE TO EFFECT THE ENDING

STUPID SENTENCES EVERYWHERE

WHO GAVE MILK

WHO MADE BEDS

WHO LIVED IN THE WOODS

WHO RAN TO THE RIVER

WHO DIED LOOKING

WHOSE THOUGHTS ARE MISSING

opposite and following two pages: From *Erlauf*. White planting, Bethel White granite walkways, and searchlight set in Bethel White granite column; light: approximately 1 mile high. Permanent installation, Erlauf, Austria, 1995.

DISCARD OBJECTS
SWALLOW CHATTER
SCORN HOPE
CHOKE SOBS
CONSTANCY
SCORN

CHRONOLOGY

1950
Born on July 29 in Gallipolis, Ohio, the oldest of three children, to Richard V. and Virginia B. Holzer. Family moves to Lancaster, Ohio.

1961
Makes her first trip to New York; visits the Metropolitan Museum of Art.

1966–68
Studies at Pine Crest Preparatory School, Fort Lauderdale, Florida.

1968–70
Takes liberal-arts program at Duke University, Durham, North Carolina, and summer art classes at Ohio University.

1970–71
Pursues drawing, printmaking, and liberal-arts courses at University of Chicago, and summer art classes at Ohio University.

1972–73
Attends Ohio University; receives B.F.A. in painting and printmaking. Visits New York following graduation, staying in an apartment downtown, on 13th Street.

1973
Travels to Europe for the first time; visits Musée du Louvre, Paris, Museo Nacional del Prado, Madrid, and Museu Picasso, Barcelona.

1974
Attends summer session at Rhode Island School of Design, Providence; meets fellow student Mike Glier.

1974–75
Models for fine-arts classes at RISD.

1975–76
Begins M.F.A. program in painting at RISD. Works as a graduate assistant for undergraduate classes and as a hot walker at Lincoln Downs horse racetrack. Uses words in her paintings.

1977
After being accepted into the Whitney Museum of American Art's Independent Study Program, moves to Great Jones Street in New York. Receives M.F.A. from RISD. Starts writing *Truisms*; has typewritten texts reproduced as posters, which she puts up around Manhattan.

1978
Photostats and audiotape of *Truisms* are presented in window of Franklin Furnace, New York. Waitresses at Spring Street Bar.

1979–80
Works as a typesetter at Daniel Shapiro's The Old Typosopher shop, New York. Organizes *Manifesto Show* with Colen Fitzgibbon at 5 Bleecker Street, New York, marking the beginning of her involvement with the artists' group Collaborative Projects (Colab). With Stephen Eins, opens Fashion Moda in the Bronx, a store that sells inexpensive artist-made objects. Puts up posters of *Inflammatory Essays* around Manhattan.

1980–82
Works as a typesetter for *Laundry News* and *Direct Marketing Newsletter* in New York. *Truisms* are printed on T-shirts. Collaborates with artist Peter Nadin on the *Living* series, some of which appear in self-published books and on metal plaques. The series is shown at Barbara Gladstone Gallery, New York, Holzer's first show at the gallery.

1981
Participates in first international exhibition, *Heute, Westkunst: Zeitgenössische Kunst seit 1939*, Museen der Stadt Köln and Messegelände Rheinhallen, Cologne; shows the *Living* series.

1982
At the invitation of Public Art Fund, Inc., New York, displays *Truisms* on the Spectacolor sign in Times Square, her first use of an electronic sign. Finds LED signs in New York through the yellow pages and begins to work with them extensively. Shows *Truisms* and *Inflammatory Essays* at *Documenta 7*, Kassel.

1984
Marries Mike Glier on May 21. Texts from the *Survival* series appear on silver and black stickers, and,

sometimes accompanied by computer-generated illustrations, on UNEX electronic signs. Organizes *Sign on a Truck*, a large video-compatible screen on the back of a truck, on which artists' videos on the subject of the forthcoming presidential election are shown, along with live footage of members of the audience being interviewed by an MC; the truck appears at two outdoor locations in New York.

1985–86
Moves to Hoosick Falls, New York. Creates texts and first granite benches for the *Under a Rock* series. Begins to work with Sunrise Systems for electronic signs and Rutland Marble and Granite for stonework. Texts from the *Survival* series appear on tractor hats.

1986
During the exhibition *Subversive Acts: Artists Working with the Media Politically*, University of New Mexico Art Museum, Albuquerque, and Art Gallery, Fogelson Library Center, College of Santa Fe, a text from the *Survival* series is shown on Albuquerque television as a public-service announcement. For *Protect Me from What I Want*, an exhibition organized by the Nevada Institute for Contemporary Art, University of Nevada at Las Vegas, texts appear on five electronic signs around Las Vegas.

1987
First sarcophagi, accompanied by LED signs with texts from *Laments*, premiere at *Documenta 8*, Kassel.

1988
Daughter, Lili, is born on May 22. Selected by seven members of the Advisory Committee for Major International Exhibitions to represent the United States at the *Biennale di Venezia* in 1990. *Art Breaks*—short segments featuring texts from *Truisms*, the *Living* series, and the *Survival* series— are aired at random intervals on the cable-television channel MTV.

1989–90
The *Laments* are shown on thirteen stone sarcophagi and thirteen synchronized LED signs at the Dia Art Foundation, New York. A selection of all texts to date appear on a helical LED sign on the parapet of the Solomon R. Guggenheim Museum; benches inscribed with *Survival* texts form a circle on the rotunda floor,

and benches with *Living* texts are installed in rows in the High Gallery.

1990–91
Represents the United States at the *XLIV Biennale di Venezia*; *Mother and Child* texts and other selected writings appear on LED signs and are inscribed in marble benches and floors. The installation wins the Leone d'Oro for best pavilion and tours museums in Europe and the United States.

1991
LED signs are permanently installed in the Ludwig Museum, Aachen, Germany. Similar permanent electronic pieces will follow at Toyota Municipal Museum of Art, Toyota, Japan (1995), Schiphol Airport, Amsterdam (1996), and Hamburger Kunsthalle, Hamburg (1996).

1992–93
The *War* text is shown on LED signs at Kunsthalle Basel and at church of St. Peter in Cologne.

1993
Creates *Lustmord* texts, describing the rape and murder of women in war, for a project in *Süddeutsche Zeitung Magazin*, Munich; photographs of the texts handwritten on skin are reproduced inside the magazine, while the cover features texts printed in ink made from human blood. The project is awarded a Gold Medal for Title and a Gold Medal for Design by the Art Directors Club of Europe. At the Guggenheim Museum SoHo, two virtual-reality works, based on the *Lustmord* texts and created in collaboration with Sense8 and Intel, are shown as part of *Virtual Reality: An Emerging Medium*.

1994
Lustmord texts are shown at Barbara Gladstone Gallery: on a volumetric electronic sign that creates 3-D images, in the leather walls of a hutlike structure, and on silver tags that encircle human bones. A serpentine LED sign and other works are shown at Art Tower Mito, Contemporary Art Center, Mito, Japan; the show travels to Art Gallery Atrium, Fukuoka, Japan. Receives an honorary Doctorate of Arts from Ohio University, and the Skowhegan Medal for Installation from the Skowhegan School of Painting and Sculpture.

1994–95
Creates two outdoor memorials relating to World War II: BLACK GARDEN in Nordhorn, Germany, and *Erlauf Monument* in Erlauf, Austria. BLACK GARDEN incorporates black and white planting and red sandstone benches in a formal garden. *Erlauf Monument* consists of white planting, inscribed stone paths, and a searchlight.

1995
äda 'web commissions a Web site, *Please Change Beliefs*, which presents texts from *Truisms*, *Inflammatory Essays*, the *Living* series, the *Survival* series, and *Laments*, and allows the audience to access and modify the *Truisms*.

1996
Receives the Crystal Award from the World Economic Forum, Davos, Switzerland, for artists who have made an outstanding contribution to cross-cultural understanding. Laser projections of *Lustmord* and other texts are shown on the Völkerschlachtdenkmal, Leipzig, Germany, one of the largest war memorials in the world. Creates a project for Slate, an on-line magazine. Collaborates with Helmut Lang to create *I Smell You on My Skin* for the *Biennale di Firenze*, Florence: *Arno* text debuts in a xenon projection against the Palazzo Bargagli on the Arno river; selected texts also appear on taxi hoods and on hanging vertical LED signs in a *Biennale* pavilion.

SELECTED EXHIBITION HISTORY

Exhibition entries are followed by related articles and reviews.

Solo and Collaborative Exhibitions and Projects

1978
Institute for Art and Urban Resources at P.S.1, New York, *Jenny Holzer Painted Room: Special Project P.S.1*, Jan. 15–Feb. 18, 1978.

Franklin Furnace, New York, *Jenny Holzer Installation*, Dec. 12–30, 1978. Included audiotape.

1979
Fashion Moda, New York, *Fashion Moda Window*, spring 1979. Included audiotape.

Printed Matter, New York, *Printed Matter Window*, 1979. Included audiotape.

1980
Onze Rue Clavel Gallery, Paris, *Textes Positions* (with Peter Nadin), Jan. 19–Feb. 8, 1980.

Rüdiger Schöttle Gallery, Munich, *Living* (with Peter Nadin), Dec. 12, 1980–Jan. 20, 1981.

1981
Artists Space, New York, *Eating Friends* (with Peter Nadin), Jan. 9–Feb. 13, 1981.

Le Nouveau Musée, Villeurbanne, France, *Living* (with Peter Nadin), June 5–July 31, 1981.

Museum für (Sub) Kultur, Berlin, *Living* (with Peter Nadin), 1981.

1982
Galerie Chantal Crousel, Paris, *Jenny Holzer–Peter Nadin: Living*, Jan. 30–March 3, 1982.

Marine Midland Bank, 140 Broadway, New York, *Art Lobby*, organized by Lower Manhattan Cultural Council, New York, Feb. 1–5, 1982.

Times Square, New York, *Messages to the Public*, outdoor installation, organized by Public Art Fund, Inc., New York, Spectacolor electronic sign, March 15–30, 1982.

Barbara Gladstone Gallery, New York, *Plaques for Buildings: Thirty Texts from the Living Series, Cast in Bronze by Jenny Holzer and Peter Nadin*, April 28–May 22, 1982.

1983
Institute of Contemporary Arts, London, *Essays, Survival Series*, April 1–May 5, 1983.

Lisson Gallery, London, *Jenny Holzer with A-One, Mike Glier, and Lady Pink: Survival Series*, May 12–June 4, 1983.

Institute of Contemporary Art, University of Pennsylvania, Philadelphia, *Investigations 3: Jenny Holzer*, June 11–July 31, 1983. Accompanied by outdoor installation, electronic sign with incandescent bulbs, News Stand Restaurant, Centre Square, Philadelphia. Brochure, with text by Paul Marincola.

Barbara Gladstone Gallery, New York, *Jenny Holzer*, Nov. 5–Dec. 1, 1983.

Ellen Handy, "Emergence: New from the Lower East Side," *Arts Magazine* (New York) 58, no. 5 (Jan. 1984), p. 55.

Lynn Zelevansky, "New York Reviews: Jenny Holzer," *Artnews* (New York) 83, no. 1 (Jan. 1984), p. 152.

Richard Armstrong, "Reviews: Jenny Holzer," *Artforum* (New York) 22, no. 6 (Feb. 1984), p. 76.

1984

Rotterdam Kunststichting, *Galerie 't Venster – Jenny Holzer–Lady Pink*, Feb. 3–April 4, 1984.

Amelie A. Wallace Gallery, State University of New York College at Old Westbury, *Jenny Holzer: Truisms and Inflammatory Essays*, March 12–31, 1984.

Sixty-sixth Street and Broadway, New York, *Graphics Change 2*, bus shelter (designed by Dennis Adams), organized by Public Art Fund, Inc., New York, April 25–July 1984.

Kunsthalle Basel, *Jenny Holzer*, May 13–June 24, 1984. Catalogue, with text by Jean-Christophe Ammann. Traveled to Le Nouveau Musée, Villeurbanne, France, Sept. 28–Dec. 16, 1984.

Dallas Museum of Art, *Jenny Holzer*, Oct. 28, 1984– Jan. 1, 1985. Brochure, with text by Sue Graze.

New York, *Sign on a Truck: A Program by Artists and Many Others on the Occasion of the Presidential Election*, outdoor installations, organized by Jenny Holzer, sponsored by Public Art Fund Inc., New York, Diamond Vision Mobile 2000 video sign, Grand Army Plaza, Nov. 3, 1984, and Bowling Green Plaza, Nov. 5, 1984.

1985

Times Square, New York, *Selection from The Survival Series*, outdoor installation, Spectacolor electronic sign, Dec. 1985–Jan. 1986.

1986

Monika Sprüth Galerie, Cologne, *Jenny Holzer*, opened April 24, 1986.

Am Hof, Vienna, *Keith Haring–Jenny Holzer*, May 10–

June 15, 1986. Catalogue, with text by Hubert Klocker and Peter Pakesch.

Palladium, New York, *Electronic Sign Project*, May 14– Nov. 15, 1986.

Galerie Crousel-Hussenot, Paris, *Jenny Holzer*, June 20–July 13, 1986.

Las Vegas, *Protect Me from What I Want*, outdoor installations, organized by Nevada Institute for Contemporary Art, University of Nevada at Las Vegas; Daktronics double-sided electronic sign, Caesars Palace, Sept. 2–8, 1986; Kellego electronic sign, Fashion Show Mall, Sept. 2–8, 1986; Mark 500 electronic sign, Thomas & Mack Center, Sept. 2–8, 1986; electronic sign, Regency Plaza, Sept. 2–8, 1986; and electronic sign, baggage carousel, McCarran International Airport, Sept. 12–28, 1986.

Barbara Gladstone Gallery, New York, *Under a Rock*, Oct. 7–Nov. 1, 1986.

Holland Cotter, "Jenny Holzer at Barbara Gladstone Gallery," *Art in America* (New York) 74, no. 12 (Dec. 1986), pp. 137–38.

Ronald Jones, "Jenny Holzer's 'Under a Rock,'" *Arts Magazine* (New York) 61, no. 5 (Jan. 1987), pp. 42–43.

Nancy Grimes, "New York Reviews: Jenny Holzer," *Artnews* (New York) 86, no. 2 (Feb. 1987), pp. 128–30.

Des Moines Art Center, *Jenny Holzer: Signs*, Dec. 5, 1986–Feb. 1, 1987. Catalogue, with text by Joan Simon and interview with the artist by Bruce Ferguson. Traveled to Aspen Art Museum, Feb. 19–April 12, 1987; Artspace, San Francisco, May 5–June 27, 1987, accompanied by outdoor installations, electronic sign, Showplace Square, May 5–June 27, 1987, and Sony JumboTRON video sign and monochrome electronic sign, Candlestick Park, May 26, 1987; Museum of Contemporary Art, Chicago, as *Options 30: Jenny Holzer*, July 31–Sept. 27, 1987; and The List Visual Arts Center at Massachusetts Institute of Technology, Cambridge, Oct. 9–Nov. 29, 1987, accompanied by outdoor installation, painted billboard, Central Square, Cambridge.

Myriam Weisang, "Getting What She Wants: Jenny Holzer Signs On in San Francisco," *San Francisco Examiner Image*, May 3, 1987, p. 31.

Kenneth Baker, "Artist's Electronic Signs Flash Around Town," *San Francisco Chronicle*, May 14, 1987, p. 1.

1987

Rhona Hoffman Gallery, Chicago, *Jenny Holzer: Under a Rock*, Feb. 13–March 21, 1987.

Hamburg, *Zwei spektakuläre Kunstaktionen der New Yorker Künstlerin Jenny Holzer im Oktober in Hamburg*, outdoor installations and public projects, Colormotion electronic sign and railway cars, Hamburger Hauptbahnhof, and broadcasts on radio station 107-FM, Oct. 1987.

Alan G. Artner, "Surprising View from Jenny Holzer," *Chicago Tribune*, Feb. 27, 1987, Section 7, p. 52.

Colin Westerbeck, "Reviews: Jenny Holzer," *Artforum* (New York) 25, no. 9 (May 1987), pp. 154–55.

1988

HoffmanBorman Gallery, Santa Monica, *Jenny Holzer*, March 11–April 9, 1988.

Christopher Knight, "Words to the Wise, Spoken to the Eyes," *Los Angeles Herald Examiner*, March 23, 1988, p. 4.

The Brooklyn Museum, *Jenny Holzer: Signs and Benches*, May 5–July 18, 1988.

Ellen Handy, "Jenny Holzer," *Arts Magazine* (New York) 63, no. 1 (Sept. 1988), p. 91.

MTV, New York, *Art Breaks*, television spots, first aired Aug. 15, 1988.

Interim Art Gallery, London, *Plaques, The Living Series 1980–82, The Survival Series 1983–85*, Nov. 27, 1988–Dec. 21, 1989.

Institute of Contemporary Arts, London, *Jenny Holzer: Signs/Under a Rock*, Dec. 7, 1988–Feb. 12, 1989, accompanied by outdoor installations, organized by The Artangel Trust, London; Metrovision electronic sign, Shaftesbury Square, Belfast, Dec. 6–31, 1988; Zakks electronic sign, Bradbury Place, Belfast, Dec. 6–31, 1988; Maiden Spectacolor electronic sign, Piccadilly Circus, London, Dec. 1988–Jan. 1989; and Mayavision video monitors, Leicester Square underground station, London, Dec. 1988. Catalogue, with texts by Iwona Blazwick and Joan Simon, and interview with the artist by Bruce Ferguson.

James Odling-Smee, "Advertising Artistry," *Fortnight* (Belfast), Dec. 1988, p. 26.

Merlin Carpenter, "Reviews: Jenny Holzer," *Artscribe International* (London), no. 74 (March–April 1989), p. 72.

James Odling-Smee, "Jenny Holzer: Bradbury Place and Shaftesbury Square, Belfast," *Circa* (Belfast), March–April 1989, pp. 36–37.

Gray Watson, "Reviews: Jenny Holzer: ICA and Elsewhere, London," *Flash Art* (Milan), no. 145 (March–April 1989), pp. 120–21.

1989
Ydessa Hendeles Art Foundation, Toronto, *Jenny Holzer*, opened Jan. 28, 1989, accompanied by outdoor installations, sponsored by Electromedia, Toronto, and Art Metropole, Toronto, Pixelboard electronic sign, 696 Yonge Street, and LED sign, 778 King Street West, Jan. 28–Feb. 28, 1989.

Dia Art Foundation, New York, *Jenny Holzer: Laments 1988–89*, March 2–June 18, 1989, and Oct. 13, 1989–Feb. 18, 1990. Videotape and artist's book, *Laments*, published by Dia Art Foundation and the artist.

Roberta Smith, "Flashing Aphorisms by Jenny Holzer at Dia," *The New York Times*, March 10, 1989, p. 26.

Nancy Princenthal, "The Quick and the Dead: Jenny Holzer's 'Laments' at Dia," *The Village Voice* (New York), March 14, 1989, pp. 31–32.

Kay Larson, "In the Beginning Was the Word," *New York Magazine*, April 3, 1989, pp. 71–72.

Hilton Kramer, "Lugubrious Jenny Holzer Exhibit at One of the City's Creepiest Spots," *The New York Observer*, April 10, 1989, pp. 1, 13.

Doris C. Freedman Plaza, New York, *Benches*, organized by Public Art Fund, Inc., New York, July 1–Dec. 31, 1989.

Michael Brenson, "Bold Sculpture for Wide-Open Spaces," *The New York Times*, July 21, 1989, pp. C1, C24.

Solomon R. Guggenheim Museum, New York, *Jenny Holzer*, Dec. 12, 1989–Feb. 25, 1990. Catalogue, with text and interview by Diane Waldman.

Roberta Smith, "Holzer Makes the Guggenheim a Museum of Many Messages," *The New York Times*, Dec. 13, 1989, p. C19.

Kay Larson, "Jenny Be Good," *New York Magazine*, Jan. 8, 1990, p. 69.

"Letters to the Editor: A Few Words from Jenny Holzer," *The New York Times Magazine*, Jan. 14, 1990, p. 6.

Robert Cauthorn, "Holzer Gives Guggenheim Flashes of Art on the Blink," *Arizona Daily Star* (Tucson), Jan. 19, 1990, p. F9.

Eleanor Heartney, "Jenny Holzer: Guggenheim Museum," *Artnews* (New York) 89, no. 3 (March 1990), p. 173.

John Miller, "Jenny Holzer: Guggenheim Museum," *Artscribe International* (London), no. 80 (March–April 1990), p. 76.

"Solomon R. Guggenheim Museum: Jenny Holzer," *The Print Collector's Newsletter* (New York), May–June 1990, pp. 64–65.

Laura Fagotti, "Una Spirale di LED al Guggenheim," *Allestire* (Milan) 10, no. 11 (Nov. 1990), pp. 49–51.

1990
United States Pavilion, *XLIV Biennale di Venezia*, Venice, May 27– Sept. 30, 1990. Catalogue, with text by Michael Auping, published by Albright-Knox Art Gallery, Buffalo (rev. ed., 1991); Danish edition published by Louisiana Museum, Humlebaek, Denmark. Traveled to Städtische Kunsthalle, Düsseldorf, Nov. 15, 1990–Jan. 1, 1991; Louisiana Museum, Humlebaek, Denmark, March 16–April 28, 1991; Albright-Knox Art Gallery, Buffalo, July 13–Sept. 1, 1991, accompanied by outdoor installations, Daktronics electronic sign, Pilot Field, Buffalo, and billboards, various locations in Buffalo, and by texts aired on PBS Channels 17 and 23; and Walker Art Center, Minneapolis, Sept. 20–Nov. 20, 1991.

Simonetta Rasponi, ed., *XLIV Esposizione Internazionale d'Arte La Biennale di Venezia: General Catalog 1990*, exh. cat. (Venice: Gruppo Editoriale Fabbri, 1990), pp. 9, 16, 221–27.

John Bentley Mays, "Venetian Visions," *Toronto Globe and Mail*, May 26, 1990, p. C15.

Michael Kimmelman, "Venice Biennale Opens with Surprises," *The New York Times*, May 28, 1990, pp. C11, C17.

Amei Wallach, "Jenny Holzer and American Pavilion Win a Grand Prize," *New York Newsday*, May 28, 1990, Section 2, p. 5.

Ingrid Sischy and Karen Marta, "Art in Venice: Holzer Has Words for America," *Interview* (New York) 20, no. 6 (June 1990), p. 92.

Michael Gibson, "From the Poetic to Kitsch at the Biennale," *International Herald Tribune* (Paris), June 2–3, 1990, p. 9.

Louisa Buck, "Artefax: Hanging in the Air," *New Statesmen and Society* (London), June 8, 1990, pp. 41–42.

Michael Kimmelman, "A Changed Biennale Remains the Same," *The New York Times*, June 10, 1990, p. H35.

Peter Plagens, "The Venice Artfest," *Newsweek* (international edition), June 11, 1990, pp. 40–41.

Lewis Kachur, "Venice Preview: Jenny Holzer," *Art International* (Paris), no. 11 (summer 1990), p. 89.

Alfred Nemeczek, "Biennale 90: Amerika verkauft sich am besten," *Art* (Hamburg), no. 7 (July 1990), pp. 28–37.

Hilton Als, "Def in Venice: Fear and Loathing at the Biennale," *The Village Voice* (New York), July 17, 1990, pp. 41–45.

Jack Flam, "Mixed-Up-Media: The Same New Thing," *The Wall Street Journal* (New York), July 25, 1990, p. A10.

Robert Hughes, "A Sampler of Witless Truisms," *Time* (New York), July 30, 1990, p. 66.

David Joselit, "Holzer: Speaking of Power," *Art in America* (New York) 78, no. 10 (Oct. 1990), pp. 155–57.

Marcia E. Vetrocq, "Vexed in Venice," *Art in America* (New York) 78, no. 10 (Oct. 1990), pp. 152–63.

1991

Ludwig Museum, Aachen, Germany, permanent installation, opened June 10, 1991.

Laura Carpenter Fine Art, Santa Fe, *Selections from The Living Series: 1980–1982*, organized in association with Barbara Gladstone Gallery, New York, Oct. 3–Dec. 12, 1991. Catalogue, *Jenny Holzer: The Living Series*, with text by Rhonda Lieberman, published by Tallgrass Press, Santa Fe, 1992. Traveled to The Claremont Graduate School, Claremont, California, opened Jan. 1992, and North Dakota Museum of Art, Grand Forks, March 15–May 17, 1992.

1992

Ydessa Hendeles Art Foundation, Toronto, *Jenny Holzer*, May 23, 1992–March 6, 1993.

1993

Center for Contemporary Art, Ujazdowski Castle, Warsaw, *Street Art: Jenny Holzer*, opened April 25, 1993.

Jolanta Ciesielska, "Jenny Holzer: Centrum Sztuki Wspólczesnej, Zamek Ujazdowski, Warsawa," *Artelier* (Poznan) 2, no. 2 (1993), pp. 34–36.

University of California, San Diego, *Green Table*, permanent installation, inaugurated March 6, 1993.

Österreichisches Museum für Angewandte Kunst, Vienna, *The Empire Style and Biedermeier Permanent Collection Installation*, permanent installation, opened May 1993.

Christian Witt-Dörring, "Designing Artist: Jenny Holzer," in Peter Noever, ed., *MAK: Austrian Museum of Applied Arts, Vienna* (second ed.; Munich: Prestel, 1995), pp. 54–55.

Church of St. Peter, Cologne, *War*, Oct. 1993.

Haus der Kunst, Munich, *Da Wo Frauen Sterben, Bin Ich Hellwach*, Nov. 16–Dec. 12, 1993.

Barry Whistler Gallery, Dallas, *The Living Series*, Nov. 19–Dec. 18, 1993.

Dallas Museum of Art, *Jenny Holzer: The Venice Installation*, Nov. 20, 1993–March 19, 1995.

1994

Bergen Billedgalleri, Bergen, Norway, *Lystmord: Jeg Er Våken På Stedet Hvor Kvinner Dør*, March 12–May 8,

1994. Catalogue, with text by Per Bjarne Boym and interview with the artist by Christian Kämmerling.

Barbara Gladstone Gallery, New York, *Lustmord, 1994*, May 5–June 30, 1994.

Holland Cotter, "Lustmord," *The New York Times*, May 13, 1994, p. C26.

Valerie Filipovna, "Truth and Truisms," *Paper* (New York) 11, no. 6 (June 1994), p. 35.

Nancy Princenthal, "Jenny Holzer at Barbara Gladstone," *Art in America* (New York) 82, no. 11 (Nov. 1994), pp. 122–23.

Art Tower Mito, Contemporary Art Center, Mito, Japan, *Jenny Holzer*, July 30–Oct. 16, 1994. Two catalogues, with texts by Eriko Osaka and Toshio Shimizu. Traveled to Art Gallery Atrium, Fukuoka, Japan, Nov. 18, 1994–Jan. 8, 1995.

Yasushi Kurabayashi, "Jenny Holzer," *GQ* (Tokyo) 10, no. 20 (Oct. 1994), pp. 178–81.

"Jenny Holzer," *Bijutsu Techo: Monthly Art Magazine* (Japan) 46, no. 698 (Dec. 1994), pp. 15–42.

Akio Nakamata, "I Enjoy Real and Unreal," *Wired* (Tokyo) 1, no. 2 (March 1995), pp. 62–65.

Nordhorn, Germany, *BLACK GARDEN*, permanent installation, inaugurated Oct. 28, 1994.

Eva Ungar Grudin, "Sichtbare Dunkelheit: Jenny Holzers Gegen-Denkmal in Nordhorn," in *Nordhorn Kulturbeiträge 4: Vom Langemarckplatz zum Schwarzen Garten* (Nordhorn: Stadt Nordhorn, Kulturdezernat, 1996), pp. 41–47.

Städtische Galerie Nordhorn, Nordhorn, Germany, *BLACK GARDEN*, Oct. 29–Nov. 27, 1994. Catalogue, with texts by Sabine Dylla and Justin Hoffmann.

1995

Monika Sprüth Galerie, Cologne, *Lustmord*, Feb. 8–April 29, 1995.

Erlauf, Austria, *Erlauf Monument*, permanent installation, inaugurated May 8, 1995. Catalogue, *Erlauf Peace Monument: Jenny Holzer/Oleg Komov*, with texts by Katharina Blaas-Pratscher, Siegwald Ganglmair, and Susanne Neuburger, published by Niederösterreichischen Landesmuseums, Vienna.

Katharina Blaas-Pratscher and Franz Kuttner, "Veroffentlichte Kunst im öffentlichen Raum," in *Raum Neiderösterreich Band 3* (Vienna: Autor Innen, 1995), pp. 64–65.

Rainer Metzger, "Ein kalter Krieg mit anderen Mitteln," *Der Standard* (Vienna), May 6–7, 1995, p. 50.

Thomas Götz, "Ein Mädchen, zwei Soldaten und das Licht," *Die Presse* (Vienna), May 8, 1995.

Henriette Horny, "Keinen Einfluß auf den Lauf der Dinge haben," *Kurier* (Vienna), May 8, 1995.

äda 'web, http://adaweb.com/cgi-bin/jfsjr/truism, *Please Change Beliefs*, on-line project, launched May 23, 1995.

Glen Helfand, "WEBReviews," *The Web Magazine*, Oct.–Nov. 1996, pp. 49–50.

Toyota Municipal Museum of Art, Toyota, Japan, *Installation for the Toyota Municipal Museum of Art*, permanent installation, opened Sept. 30, 1995.

Williams College Museum of Art, Williamstown, Massachusetts, *Jenny Holzer: From the Laments Series, 1989*, Oct. 7, 1995–Feb. 18, 1996.

Courthouse, Allentown, Pennsylvania, *Allentown Benches: Selections from the Truisms and Survival Series*, permanent installation, opened Dec. 29, 1995.

1996

Trade Fair Center, Leipzig, Germany, permanent installation, opened March 13, 1996. Catalogue, *Projekte: Kunst in der Neuen Messe Leipzig/Projects: Art at the New Trade Fair Center Leipzig*, with texts by Alex Papadopoulou, Chris Rehberger, and Tobias Rehberger, published by Brigitte Oetker and Christiane Schneider.

Völkerschlachtdenkmal, Leipzig, Germany, *KriegsZustand*, outdoor installation, organized by Leipziger Galerie für Zeitgenössische Kunst, June 14–16, 1996. Catalogue, with texts by Anne-Marie Bonnet, Eva Ungar Grudin, and Klaus Werner, published by Leipziger Galerie für Zeitgenössische Kunst, forthcoming.

Thomas Irmer, "Deutsche Denkmäler: Ein Gespräch mit Jenny Holzer," *Neue Bildende Kunst: Zeitschrift für Kunst und Kritik*, Aug.–Sept. 1996, p. 5.

Slate, http://www.antennaco.com/holzer/holzer.html., on-line project, June 24–July 10, 1996.

Galerie Rähnitzgasse der Landeshauptstadt, Dresden, *Jenny Holzer: Lustmord*, June 27–Aug. 11, 1996.

Schiphol Airport, Amsterdam, *Installation at Schiphol Airport Authority*, permanent installation, opened July 1996.

Kunstmuseum des Kantons Thurgau, Kartause Ittingen, Warth, Switzerland, *Jenny Holzer: Lustmord*, Sept. 22, 1996–April 27, 1997. Catalogue, with texts by Christian Kämmerling, Markus Landert, Beatrix Ruf, Noemi Smolik, and Yvonne Volkart.

Christoph Doswald, "Der Schmerz wird sichtbar gemacht," *Facts* (Zurich), Sept. 19, 1996, pp. 154–55.

Ludmila Vachtova, "Von der Haut bis auf die Knochen," *Die Weltwoche* (Zurich), Sept. 26, 1996, pp. 64–66.

Nicklaus Oberholzer. "Ich weiss wer du bist, und es tut mir gar nicht gut," *Neue Luzerner Zeitung* (Lucerne), Oct. 2, 1996, p. 39.

Anneliese Zwez, "Lust und Grauen in der Psyche," *Berner Rundschau* (Bern), Oct. 29, 1996, p. 25.

Ralf Beil, "Psychopathologie im Klosterkeller," *Neue Zürcher Zeitung* (Zurich), Oct. 31, 1996, pp. 48–49.

Monica Daniela Hux, "Erschreckende Normalität," *Thurgauer Zeitung* (Frauenfeld), Nov. 14, 1996, p. 13.

Hamburger Kunsthalle, Hamburg, permanent installation, opened Oct. 1996.

Group Exhibitions

1978
Los Angeles Institute of Contemporary Art, *Artwords and Bookworks: An International Exhibition of Recent Artists' Books and Ephemera*, Feb. 28–March 30, 1978. Catalogue, with texts by Mike Crane, Judith Hoffberg, and Joan Hugo. Traveled to Artists Space, New York, June 10–30, 1978; Herron School of Art, Indianapolis, Sept. 15–29, 1978; and Contemporary Arts Center, New Orleans, Oct. 14–30, 1978.

Susan C. Larson, "A Booklover's Dream," *Artnews* (New York) 77, no. 5 (May 1978), pp. 144–52.

1979
5 Bleecker Street, New York, *Manifesto Show*, early 1979.

1980
Institute of Contemporary Arts, London, *Issue: Social Strategies by Women Artists*, Nov. 14–Dec. 21, 1980. Catalogue, with texts by Margaret Harrison, Lucy R. Lippard, and Sandy Nairne.

Brooke Alexander, Inc., New York, *Collaborative Projects Presents a Benefit Exhibition at Brooke Alexander, Inc.*, Dec. 6–31, 1980.

Abandoned building, Forty-first Street and Seventh Avenue, New York, *The Times Square Show*, 1980.

Jeffrey Deitch, "Report from Times Square," *Art in America* (New York) 68, no. 7 (Sept. 1980), pp. 59–63.

1981
Chrysler Museum, Norfolk, Virginia, *Crimes of Compassion*, April 16–May 31, 1981. Catalogue, with text by Thomas W. Styron.

Museen der Stadt Köln, and Messegelände Rheinhallen, Cologne, *Heute, Westkunst: Zeitgenössische Kunst seit 1939*, May 30–Aug. 16, 1981. Catalogue, with texts by Hugo Borger, Laszlo Glozer, Kasper König, and Karl Ruhrberg.

Richard Armstrong, "Reviews: 'Heute,' Westkunst," *Artforum* (New York) 20, no. 1 (Sept. 1981), pp. 83–86.

Brooke Alexander Gallery, Inc., New York, *Represent, Representation, Representative*, Sept. 8–Oct. 3, 1981.

Annina Nosei Gallery, New York, *Public Address*, Oct. 31–Nov. 19, 1981.

1982
University Art Gallery, State University of New York at Binghamton, *Nine Women Artists*, March 27–April 25, 1982. Catalogue, with text by Josephine Gear and interviews with the artists by Jeff Allen, Eve Daniels, Tami Goodger, Robin Hatchett, Joyce Kaufman, Johanna Mustacchi, Tom Persico, Anne Marie Reilly, and Jeri Slavin.

Museum Fridericianum, Orangerie, and Neue Galerie, Kassel, *Documenta 7*, June 19–Sept. 23, 1982, accompanied by outdoor installation, painted wall, Haus Kranefuss, Kassel. Catalogue, with texts by

Jorge Luis Borges, Saskia Bos, Coosje van Bruggen, Germano Celant, Hans Eichel, T. S. Eliot, Rudi H. Fuchs, Johannes Gachnang, J. W. von Goethe, Friedrich Hölderlin, Walter Nikkels, Gerhard Storck, and the artists.

American Graffiti Gallery, Amsterdam, *Jenny Holzer, Lee, Aron Fink*, Sept.–Oct. 1982.

1983
Musée des Beaux-Arts de Dijon, *Présence discrète*, Jan. 10–Feb. 28, 1983.

Protetch/McNeil, New York, *The Revolutionary Power of Women's Laughter*, Jan. 15–Feb. 25, 1983. Brochure, with text by Jo Anna Isaak. Traveled to Arts Cultural Resource Center, Toronto, Feb. 4–28, 1983.

Jane Weinstock, "A Lass, a Laugh and a Lad," *Art in America* (New York) 71, no. 6 (summer 1983), pp. 7–10.

Whitney Museum of American Art, New York, *1983 Biennial Exhibition*, March 24–May 22, 1983. Catalogue, with texts by Tom Armstrong, John G. Hanhardt, Barbara Haskell, Richard Marshall, and Patterson Sims.

Allen Memorial Art Museum, Oberlin College, Ohio, *Art and Social Change, U.S.A.*, April 19–May 30, 1983. Catalogue, with texts by David Deitcher, Jerry Kearns, Lucy R. Lippard, William Olander, Craig Owens, and Richard E. Spear.

Institute of Contemporary Art, Boston, *Currents*, Sept. 17–Oct. 20, 1983. Brochure, with text by David Joselit.

Stedelijk Van Abbemuseum, Eindhoven, *Walter Dahn, René Daniels, Isa Genzken, Jenny Holzer, Robert Longo, Henk Visch*, Oct. 14–Nov. 20, 1983. Catalogue, with text by Rudi H. Fuchs.

Greenville County Museum of Art, Greenville, South Carolina, *From the Streets*, Oct. 25–Nov. 20, 1983.

Fine Arts Museum of Long Island, Hempstead, New York, *Written Imagery Unleashed in the Twentieth Century*, Nov. 6, 1983–Jan. 22, 1984. Catalogue, with text by Eleanor Flomenhaft.

1984

Institute for Art and Urban Resources at P.S.1, New York, *Time Line*, Jan. 22–March 18, 1984.

Gallerie Engström, Stockholm, *1984: Women in New York*, April 4–May 13, 1984. Brochure, with text by Alanna Heiss.

Art Gallery of New South Wales, and Ivan Dougherty Gallery, Sydney, *The Fifth Biennale of Sydney: Private Symbol, Social Metaphor*, April 11–June 17, 1984. Catalogue, with texts by Franco Belgiorno-Nettis, Paula Latos-Valier, Stuart Morgan, Leon Paroissien, Annelie Pohlen, Jean-Louis Pradel, Carter Ratcliff, and Nelly Richard.

Amerika Haus, Berlin, *Women of Influence*, June 12–July 28, 1984. Catalogue, with texts by Ronnie Cohen, Peter E. Haaren, Emily Hicks, Marcolo McCormick, Ronald J. Onorato, Dean Savard, and Britta Schmitz.

San Francisco Museum of Modern Art, *The Human Condition: Biennial III*, June 28–Aug. 26, 1984. Catalogue, with texts by Achille Bonito Oliva, Shirley Davis, Wolfgang Max Faust, Henry T. Hopkins, Edward Kienholz, Dorothy Martinson, and Klaus Ottman.

Städtische Kunsthalle, Düsseldorf, *Ein Anderes Klima: Aspekte der Schönheit in der zeitgenössischen Kunst/ A Different Climate: Aspects of Beauty in Contemporary Art*, Aug. 5–Oct. 5, 1984. Catalogue, with texts by Art Buchwald, Jürgen Harten, Friedrich Nicolai, and the artists.

Hirshhorn Museum and Sculpture Garden, Smithsonian Institution, Washington, D.C., *Content: A Contemporary Focus 1974–1984*, Oct. 4, 1984–Jan. 6, 1985. Catalogue, with texts by Howard N. Fox, Abram Lerner, Miranda McClintick, and Phyllis Rosenzweig.

Knight Gallery, Spirit Square Art Center, Charlotte, North Carolina, *Holzer Kruger Prince*, Nov. 28, 1984–Jan. 20, 1985. Catalogue, with texts by William Olander and Ann Shengold.

1985

Los Angeles Institute of Contemporary Art, *Secular Attitudes*, Feb. 15–March 23, 1985. Catalogue, with texts by Kathy Rae Huffman and Bob Smith.

Milwaukee Art Center, *Currents 7: Words in Action*, March 7–June 2, 1985.

Galeries Nationales du Grand Palais, Paris, *Nouvelle Biennale de Paris*, March 21–May 21, 1985. Catalogue, with texts by Achille Bonito Oliva, Georges Boudaille, Pierre Courcelles, Jean-Pierre Faye, Gérald Gassiot-Talabot, Alanna Heiss, Marie Luise Syring, and the artists.

The New Museum of Contemporary Art, New York, *Signs*, April 27–July 7, 1985. Catalogue, with text by Ned Rifkin.

Barbara Gladstone Gallery, New York, *Social Studies*, June 8–July 26, 1985.

Islip Art Museum, East Islip, New York, *Writing on the Wall*, Sept. 8–Oct. 20, 1985.

Museum of Art, Carnegie Institute, Pittsburgh, *1985 Carnegie International*, Nov. 9, 1985–Jan. 5, 1986. Catalogue, with texts by Achille Bonito Oliva, Bazon Brock, Benjamin H. D. Buchloh, John Caldwell, Germano Celant, Hal Foster, Rudi H. Fuchs, Johannes Gachnang, Per Kirkeby, Jannis Kounellis, Hilton Kramer, Donald B. Kuspit, John R. Lane, Thomas McEvilley, Mark Rosenthal, Peter Schjeldahl, and Nicholas Serota.

Monika Sprüth Galerie, Cologne, *Eau de Cologne II*, Nov. 15–Dec. 12, 1985. Catalogue, with texts by Patrick Frey, Ulla Frohne, Jo Anna Isaak, Christiane Meyer-Thoss, Stuart Morgan, Mary Anne Staniszewski, Paul Taylor, and the artists, and interviews with curators, gallerists, and critics by Judith Black, Esther Schipper, and Monika Sprüth.

Musée d'Art Contemporain de Montréal, *Ecrans Politiques*, Nov. 17, 1985–Jan. 12, 1986.

Nexus Contemporary Art Center, Atlanta, *The Public Art Show*, Nov. 23–Dec. 21, 1985. Catalogue, with texts by Ronald Jones and Milan Kundera.

Institute of Contemporary Art, Boston, *Dissent: The Issue of Modern Art in Boston, The Expressionist Challenge*, Dec. 5, 1985–Feb. 9, 1986; *Revolt in Boston, Fear vs. Freedom*, Feb. 18–April 20, 1986; and *As Found*, April 29–June 22, 1986. Catalogue, with texts by Benjamin H. D. Buchloh, Serge Guilbaut, Reinhold Heller, David Joselit, David Ross, and Elisabeth Sussman.

1986

North Gallery, University of New Mexico Art Museum, Albuquerque, and Art Gallery, Fogelson Library Center, College of Santa Fe, *Subversive Acts: Artists Working with the Media Politically*, Jan. 7–Feb. 23 and Feb. 13–31, 1986, respectively. Accompanied by public project, organized by Art/Media New Mexico, public-service announcement from the *Survival* series, aired on KNME-TV and KGGM-TV, Albuquerque, and poster with selections from *Truisms* in *Impact: Albuquerque Journal Magazine*, Jan. 28, 1986, pp. 7, 10.

> Kathleen Shields, "Exhibit Harks Back to Conceptual Art," *Albuquerque Journal*, Jan. 19, 1986, p. E2.

Art Gallery, Fogelson Library Center, College of Santa Fe, *Tuning In*, Jan. 17–31, 1986. Traveled to Museum of Fine Arts, Santa Fe, Feb. 11–March 10, 1986.

The Contemporary Arts Center, Cincinnati, *Jenny Holzer, Cindy Sherman: Personae*, Feb. 7–March 15, 1986. Catalogue, with texts by Dennis Barrie and Sarah Rogers-Lafferty.

The Corcoran Gallery of Art, Washington, D.C., *In Other Words*, May 9–June 29, 1986. Accompanied by outdoor installation, electronic sign, Dupont Circle, Washington, D.C. Catalogue, with text by Ned Rifkin.

Castello dell'Ovo, Naples, *Rooted Rhetoric: Una Tradizione nell'Arte Americana*, July 1986. Catalogue, with texts by Benjamin H. D. Buchloh, Gabriele Guercio, Joseph Kosuth, Thomas Lawson, Charles Le Vine, David Robbins, and Angelo Trimarco.

The Israel Museum, Jerusalem, *Jenny Holzer/Barbara Kruger*, Aug. 5–Oct. 5, 1986. Catalogue, with text by Suzanne Landau.

Frankfurter Kunstverein and Kunsthalle Schirn, Frankfurt, *Prospekt 86: Eine internationale Ausstellung aktueller Kunst*, Sept. 9–Nov. 11, 1986. Catalogue, with texts by Hilmar Hoffmann, Peter Weiermair, and the artists.

Centre Cultural de la Fundació Caixa de Pensions, Barcelona, *Art and Its Double: A New York Perspective/ El Arte y su doble: Una perspectiva de Nueva York*, organized by Sala de Exposiciónes de la Fundación Caja de Pensiones, Madrid, Nov. 27, 1986–Jan. 11, 1987. Catalogue, with texts by Dan Cameron and excerpts from previously published texts by Clement Greenberg, Harold Rosenberg, William Rubin,

Brian Wallis, the artists, et al. Traveled to Sala de Exposiciónes de la Fundación Caja de Pensiones, Madrid, Feb. 6–March 22, 1987.

1987
Hillwood Art Gallery, C. W. Post Center, Long Island University, Greenvale, New York, *Perverted by Language*, Feb. 11–March 6, 1987. Catalogue, with texts by Robert Nickas and the artists.

Yale University Art Gallery, New Haven, *Contemporary American Artists in Print*, March 25–May 31, 1987. Brochure, with texts by Matthew J. W. Drutt, Richard S. Field, Laura Katzman, and Ainlay Samuels.

Musée National d'Art Moderne, Centre Georges Pompidou, Paris, *L'Epoque, La Mode, La Morale, La Passion*, May 2–Aug. 17, 1987. Accompanied by outdoor installation, Centre Georges Pompidou, *Sign on a Truck*, Diamond Vision Mobile 2000 video sign, May 19–25, 1987. Catalogue, with text by Bernard Ceysson and excerpts from previously published texts by Kenneth Baker, Benjamin H. D. Buchloh, Germano Celant, Hal Foster, Fredric Jameson, Rosalind Krauss, et al.

Museum Fridericianum, Kassel, *Documenta 8*, June 12–Sept. 20, 1987. Catalogue, with texts by Manfred Beilharz, Karl Oskar Blase, Bazon Brock, Hans Eichel, Michael Erlhoff, Vittorio Fagone, Edward F. Fry, Michael Grauer and Wenzel Jacob, Wulf Herzögenrath, Elisabeth Jappe, Georg Jappe, Heinrich Klotz, Vladimir Lalo Nikolic, Pierre Restany, Lothar Romain, Manfred Schneckenburger, and Klaus Schöning.

Westfälisches Landesmuseum für Kunst und Kulturgeschichte, Münster, *Skulptur Projekte in Münster*, June 14–Oct. 4, 1987. Catalogue, with texts by Carl Andre, Klaus Bussmann, Georg Jappe, Kasper König, and Ludwig Wittgenstein.

Centre International d'Art Contemporain de Montréal, *Stations*, Aug. 1–Nov. 2, 1987. Catalogue, with texts by Roger Bellemare, James D. Campbell, Claude Gosselin, and Jacques E. Lefebvre.

The Bourse, Philadelphia, *Independence Sites: Sculpture for Public Spaces*, Aug. 6–Oct. 12, 1987. Catalogue, with texts by Stephen Berg, Paula Marincola, and Vicki Garfield Solot.

Michael McGettigan, "Putting It in Writing," *Philadephia City Paper*, Aug. 7–14, 1987, pp. 7, 16.

Amsterdam, *Century '87: Kunst van nu ontmoet Amsterdams verleden/Today's Art Face to Face with Amsterdam's Past*, Aug. 7–Sept. 14, 1987. Catalogue, with texts by J.Th. Balk, Willem Ellenbroek, Sjarel Ex, Nicolette Gast, Els Hoek, and Wendie Shaffer, and supplement of viewer with images on disks.

Saint Louis Gallery of Contemporary Art, *At Issue: Art and Advocacy*, Sept. 9–Oct. 17, 1987. Brochure, with text by Susan Walker.

Everson Museum of Art, Syracuse, *Computers in Art*, Sept. 18–Nov. 8, 1987. Catalogue, with text by Cynthia Goodman. Traveled to The Contemporary Arts Center, Cincinnati, Nov. 27, 1987–Jan. 9, 1988; IBM Gallery of Science and Art, New York, April 26–June 18, 1988; and Center for the Fine Arts, Miami, Aug. 13–Sept. 25, 1988.

Galerie Crousel-Robelin, Paris, *Jenny Holzer, Louise Lawler, Ken Lum*, Oct. 17–Nov. 17, 1987.

1988
Scott Hanson Gallery, New York, *Media Post Media*, Jan. 6–Feb. 9, 1988. Catalogue, with texts by Tricia Collins and Richard Milazzo.

The Museum of Modern Art, New York, *Committed to Print: An Exhibition of Recent American Printed Art with Social and Political Themes*, Jan. 31–April 19, 1988. Catalogue, with text by Deborah Wye.

Sidney Janis Gallery, New York, *60s/80s: Sculpture Parallels*, Feb. 25–March 6, 1988.

Bank of Boston, Boston, *The Multiple Object: European and American Sculptural Works Made in Editions*, March 7–May 31, 1988.

Boca Raton Museum of Art, Florida, *After Street Art*, April 29–May 29, 1988.

Point State Park, Pittsburgh, *Sculpture at the Point* (part of Three Rivers Arts Festival), May 15–June 26, 1988. Catalogue, with texts by John R. Brice, Gary Garrels, Jack Reynolds, and the artists.

Art Gallery of New South Wales, and Pier 2/3, Sydney, *1988 Australian Biennale: From the Southern Cross, A View of World Art c. 1940–88*, May 18–July 3, 1988. Catalogue, with texts by Franco Belgiorno-Nettis, Bernard Blistène, Ian Burn, Jürgen Habermas, Frances Lindsay, Terence Maloon, Peter Sarah, Diane Waldman, and Nick Waterlow and excerpts from previously

published texts by Bernard Blistène, Jean-Pierre Bordaz, Robert L. Pincus, John Russell, et al. Traveled to National Gallery of Victoria, Melbourne, Aug. 4–Sept. 18, 1988.

Wembley Stadium, London, *Nelson Mandela Seventieth Birthday Tribute*, June 11, 1988.

Whitney Museum of American Art Downtown at Federal Plaza, New York, *Modes of Address: Language in Art since 1960*, July 29–Sept. 23, 1988. Brochure, with texts by Thomas Hardy, Amy Heard, Ingrid Periz, and Michael Waldron.

The Guiness Hop Store and The Royal Hospital, Dublin, *ROSC '88*, Aug. 20–Oct. 15 and Aug. 21–Oct. 15, 1988, respectively. Catalogue, with texts by Aidan Dunne, Olle Granath, Rosemarie Mulcahy, Patrick J. Murphy, and Angelica Zander Rudenstine.

Third Eye Centre, Glasgow, *Camouflage*, Sept. 3–Oct. 1, 1988. Catalogue, with texts by James Bustard, Richard Kearton, and Norman Wilkinson. Traveled to Inverness Museum and Art Gallery, Glasgow, Nov. 4–Dec. 3, 1988; Stirling Smith Museum and Art Gallery, Glasgow, Dec. 10, 1988–Jan. 8, 1989; and Maclaurin Art Gallery, Ayr, Jan. 16–Feb. 11, 1989.

1989
Carleton Art Gallery, Carleton College, Northfield, Minnesota, *What Does She Want?: Current Feminist Art from the First Bank Collection*, Jan. 7–March 12, 1989. Catalogue, with texts by Nathan Braulwck, Dale K. Haworth, Lynne Sowder, and the artists. Traveled to Women's Art Registry of Minnesota, Minneapolis, April 8–May 13, 1989.

Gallery 400, The University of Illinois at Chicago, *The Presence of Absence: New Installations*, organized by Independent Curators Incorporated, New York, Jan. 11–Feb. 17, 1989. Catalogue, with text by Nina Felshin, published by Independent Curators Incorporated. Traveled to University of Arizona Museum of Art, Tucson, Feb. 22–March 29, 1989; Laumeier Sculpture Park and Garden, Saint Louis, March 18–May 29, 1989; Virginia Beach Center for the Arts, Virginia Beach, Virginia, Sept. 1–Oct. 13, 1989; Albany Institute of History and Art, Albany, New York, Sept. 23–Nov. 5, 1989; Oakville Galleries, Gairloch Gallery, Oakville, Ontario, Nov. 4–Dec. 31, 1989; University of Hawaii Art Gallery, Honolulu,

Jan. 14–Feb. 21, 1990; University of Kentucky Art Museum, Lexington, Kentucky, Jan. 14–March 4, 1990; Longview Museum and Arts Center, Longview, Texas, March 10–April 21, 1990; Prichard Art Gallery, University of Idaho, Moscow, March 16–April 29, 1990; Palmer Museum of Art, Pennsylvania State University, University Park, Aug. 26–Oct. 14, 1990; The University of Iowa Museum of Art, Iowa City, Oct. 6–Nov. 30, 1990; University Art Museum, University of New Mexico, Albuquerque, Oct. 28–Dec. 21, 1990; Florida Gulf Coast Art Center, Belleair, Jan. 8–March 3, 1991; Alberta College of Art, Calgary, Jan. 17–Feb. 17, 1991; Edna Carlsten Gallery, University of Wisconsin, Stevens Point, March 17–April 18, 1991; CU Art Galleries, University of Colorado, Boulder, June 24– Aug. 17, 1991; Palm Beach Community College Museum of Art, Lakewood, Florida, Sept. 6–Oct. 25, 1991; Surrey Art Gallery, Surrey Arts Centre, Surrey, British Columbia, Oct. 11–Nov. 22, 1991; Missoula Museum of Art, Missoula, Montana, Nov. 8, 1991– Jan. 3, 1992; Otis/Parsons Gallery, Los Angeles, Dec. 14, 1991–Feb. 7, 1992; Richard F. Brush Gallery, St. Lawrence University, Canton, New York, Jan. 21– Feb. 21, 1992; and Edwin A. Ulrich Museum of Art, The Wichita State University, Wichita, Kansas, April 22–June 14, 1992.

Tony Shafrazi Gallery, New York, *Words*, Jan. 21– Feb. 18, 1989.

Cincinnati Art Museum, *Making Their Mark: Women Artists Move into the Mainstream, 1970–85*, organized by Pennsylvania Academy of the Fine Arts, Philadelphia, Feb. 22–April 2, 1989. Catalogue, with texts by Catherine C. Brawer, Ellen G. Landau, Thomas McEvilley, Ferris Olin, Randy Rosen, Judith Stein, Calvin Tomkins, Marcia Tucker, and Ann-Sargent Wooster. Traveled to New Orleans Museum of Art, May 6–June 18, 1989; Denver Art Museum, July 22– Sept. 10, 1989; and Pennsylvania Academy of Fine Arts, Philadelphia, Oct. 20–Dec. 31, 1989.

Monika Sprüth Galerie, Cologne, *Scripta Manent — Verba Volant*, Feb. 24–April 24, 1989.

Collett Art Gallery, Weber State College, Ogden, Utah, *Recent Acquisitions*, April 7–May 5, 1989. Catalogue, with text by Henry Barendse.

The Museum of Contemporary Art, Los Angeles, *A Forest of Signs: Art in the Crisis of Representation*, May 7–Aug. 13, 1989. Catalogue, with texts by Ann Goldstein, Mary Jane Jacob, Anne Rorimer, and Howard Singerman.

Esther Schipper, Cologne, *Genetics*, May 25–June 30, 1989.

Walker Art Center, Minneapolis, *First Impressions: Early Prints by Forty-Six Contemporary Artists*, June 4– Sept. 10, 1989. Catalogue, with texts by Elizabeth Armstrong and Sheila McGuire. Traveled to Laguna Art Museum, Dec. 2, 1989–Jan. 21, 1990; Baltimore Museum of Art, Feb. 25–April 22, 1990; and Neuberger Museum, State University of New York at Purchase, June 21–Sept. 16, 1990.

Art Gallery of Ontario, Toronto, *International Contemporary Art: Selected Recent Acquisitions and Promised Gifts*, June 20–Aug. 13, 1989.

Madison Art Center, Wisconsin, *Coming of Age: Twenty-one Years of Collecting by the Madison Art Center*, Sept. 9–Nov. 12, 1989. Catalogue, with text by Janet Ela.

Whitney Museum of American Art, New York, *Image World: Art and Media Culture*, Nov. 9, 1989–Feb. 18, 1990. Catalogue, with texts by John G. Hanhardt, Marvin Heiferman, and Lisa Phillips.

1990
Fundació Caixa de Pensions, Sala de Exposiciones de la Calle Montcada, Barcelona, *Time Span: Jenny Holzer, On Kawara, Bruce Nauman, Lawrence Weiner*, Jan. 19– Feb. 25, 1990.

"Time Span," *Quaderns: Fundació Caixa de Pensions*, no. 45 (April 1990), pp. 32–33.

Hirshhorn Museum and Sculpture Garden, Smithsonian Institution, Washington, D.C., *Culture and Commentary: An Eighties Perspective*, Feb. 8–May 6, 1990. Catalogue, with texts by Maurice Culot, Kathy Halbreich, Simon Watney, et al.

Hallwalls Contemporary Arts Center, Buffalo, *Insect Politics: Body Horror/Social Order*, March 17–April 13, 1990. Catalogue, with texts by Jürgen Bruning, Stephen Derrickson, and Hank Hyena.

Haggerty Museum of Art, Marquette University, Milwaukee, *Images of Death in Contemporary Art*, March 22–June 3, 1990. Catalogue, with texts by Kit Basquin, Curtis L. Carter, and Peter Halley.

Stedelijk Museum, Amsterdam, *Energieën*, April 8– July 29. Catalogue, with text by Wim Beeren.

Wessel O'Connor, New York, *The Power of Childhood*, May 2–June 9, 1990.

Barbara Krakow Gallery, Boston, *Constructive Anger*, May 5–30, 1990.

The Art Institute of Chicago, *Affinities and Intuition: The Gerald S. Elliott Collection of Contemporary Art*, May 12–July 29, 1990. Catalogue, with texts by Michael Auping, Neal Benezra, Lynne Cooke, et al., published in association with Thames and Hudson, New York.

The New Museum of Contemporary Art, New York, May 12–Aug. 19, 1990, The Studio Museum in Harlem, New York, May 18–Aug. 19, 1990, and the Museum of Contemporary Hispanic Art, New York, May 16– Aug. 19, 1990, *The Decade Show: Frameworks of Identity in the 1980's*. Catalogue, with texts by Kinshasha Holman Conwill, Eunice Lipton, Nilda Peraza, et al.

Long Beach Museum of Art, Long Beach, California, *Video Poetics*, May 13–June 17, 1990. Catalogue, with text by Michael Nash. Accompanied by selections from *Truisms*, the *Living* series, and the *Survival* series, aired on KCOP-TV and KTLA-TV, Los Angeles, May 13–19, 1990, and on KCTV-Channel 19, Santa Barbara, Peralta Colleges Television, Oakland, Berkeley, and Alameda, and Viacom Cablevision, Marin County, May 14–20, 1990.

Milwaukee Art Museum, *Word as Image: American Art 1960–1990*, June 15–Aug. 26, 1990. Catalogue, with texts by Gerry Biller, Russell Bowman, and Dean Sobel. Traveled to Oklahoma City Art Museum, Oklahoma City, Nov. 17, 1990–Feb. 2, 1991, and Contemporary Arts Museum, Houston, Feb. 23–May 12, 1991.

Israel Museum, Jerusalem, *Life-Size: A Sense of the Real in Recent Art*, Sept. 1990. Catalogue, with text by Suzanne Landau.

Museum Wiesbaden, Wiesbaden, Germany, *Künstlerinnen des 20. Jahrhunderts*, Sept. 1–Nov. 25, 1990. Catalogue, with texts by Volker Rattemeyer, Ludmila Vachtova, Barbara Wally, et al.

The Museum of Modern Art, New York, *High & Low: Modern Art and Popular Culture*, Oct. 7, 1990–Jan. 15, 1991. Catalogue, with texts by Adam Gopnik and Kirk Varnedoe. Traveled to The Art Institute of Chicago, Feb. 20–May 12, 1991, and The Museum of Contemporary Art, Los Angeles, June 21–Sept. 15, 1991.

Espace Electra, Paris, *Nature (Artificielle)*, Oct. 9–Dec. 30, 1990. Catalogue, with texts by Marcel Boiteux and Anne Tronche.

Aldrich Museum of Contemporary Art, Ridgefield, Connecticut, *Language in Art*, Oct. 20, 1990–Jan. 6, 1991.

Grande Galerie, Centre Georges Pompidou, Paris, *Art & Pub: Art et Publicité 1890–1990*, Oct. 31, 1990–Feb. 25, 1991. Catalogue, with texts by Jean-Hubert Martin, Anne Baldassari, François Burkhardt, et al.

1991
Andrea Rosen Gallery, New York, *Video Library*, Jan. 11–March 23, 1991.

John Weber Gallery, New York, *The Political Arm*, organized by Washington University Gallery of Art, Saint Louis, Feb. 1–23, 1991. Catalogue, with text by Joseph D. Ketner and Chris Scoates. Traveled to Washington University Gallery of Art, Saint Louis, June 8–Aug. 11, 1991.

Duke University Museum of Art, Durham, North Carolina, *Contemporary Art from the Collection of Jason Rubell*, March 1–May 19, 1991. Catalogue, with texts by Michael P. Mezzatesta and Jason Rubell.

Brooke Alexander Editions, New York, *Poets/Painters Collaborations: A Benefit Exhibition and Sale for the Poetry Project*, March 14–30, 1991.

Museum of Contemporary Art, Wright State University, Dayton, Ohio, *Words & #s*, April 7–May 10, 1991. Catalogue, with texts by Carol A. Nathanson and Barry A. Rosenberg.

Galerie Metropol, Vienna, *The Picture After the Last Picture*, April 15–June 15, 1991. Catalogue, with texts by Jean-Christophe Ammann, Jean Baudrillard, Benjamin H. D. Buchloh, et al. Traveled to Museum Voor Hedendaagse Kunst Het Krulthuls, Hertogenbosch, The Netherlands, Nov. 17, 1991–Jan. 5, 1992.

Martin-Gropius-Bau, Berlin, *Metropolis*, April 20–July 21, 1991. Catalogue, with texts by Christos M. Joachimides and Norman Rosenthal.

Anne Plumb Gallery, New York, *Show of Strength: A Sale of Works by Today's Outstanding Women Artists in Support of Madre*, April 27–May 4, 1991.

Centraal Museum, Utrecht, The Netherlands, *Nachtregels/Night Lines: Words Without Thoughts Never to Heaven Go*, April 27–Oct. 15, 1991. Catalogue, with texts by Sjarel Ex and Bert Jansen.

> Jan Brand, Nicolette Gast, and Robert-Jan Muller, eds., *De Woorden en de Beelden/The Words and the Images: Text and Image in the Art of the Twentieth Century* (Utrecht: Centraal Museum, 1991), pp. 191–205, 260–66.

San Jose Museum of Art, *Compassion and Protest: Recent Social and Political Art from the Eli Broad Family Foundation Collection*, June 1–Aug. 25, 1991. Catalogue, with texts by David Cateforis, Michael Danoff, Michelle Meyers, et al.

Setagaya Art Museum, Tokyo, *Beyond the Frame: American Art 1960–1990*, July 6–Aug. 18, 1991. Traveled to National Museum of Art, Osaka, Aug. 29–Sept. 29, 1991, and Fukuoka Art Museum, Fukuoka, Nov. 15–Dec. 15, 1991.

Indianapolis Museum of Art, *Power: Its Myths and Mores in American Art, 1961–1991*, Sept. 5–Nov. 3, 1991. Catalogue, with texts by Anna C. Chave, Holliday T. Day, George E. Marcus, Catsou Roberts, and Brian Wallis, published in cooperation with Indiana University Press. Traveled to Akron Art Museum, Jan. 18–March 21, 1992, and Virginia Museum of Fine Arts, Richmond, May 11–July 12, 1992.

International Center of Photography, New York, *Speechless Text/Image Video*, Sept. 6–Nov. 17, 1991.

Serpentine Gallery, London, *Objects for the Ideal Home*, Sept. 11–Oct. 20, 1991. Catalogue, *Objects for the Ideal Home: The Legacy of Pop Art*, with texts by Marco Livingstone, Julia Peyton-Jones, and Andrea Schlicker.

Institute of Contemporary Art, University of Pennsylvania, Philadelphia, *Devil on the Stairs: Looking Back on the Eighties*, Oct. 4, 1991–Jan. 5, 1992. Catalogue, with texts by Peter Schjeldahl and Robert Storr. Traveled to Newport Harbor Art Museum,

Newport Beach, California, April 16–June 21, 1992.

Fraenkel Gallery, San Francisco, *In a Dream*, Oct. 24–Nov. 11, 1991.

Paula Cooper Gallery, New York, *Act-Up Benefit Art Sale*, Dec. 5–21, 1991.

1992
Barbara Gladstone Gallery, New York, *c. 1980*, Jan. 18–Feb. 22, 1992.

The Museum of Modern Art, New York, *Allegories of Modernism: Contemporary Drawing*, Feb. 12–May 12, 1992. Catalogue, with text by Bernice Rose.

Hayward Gallery, London, *Doubletake: Collective Memory and Current Art*, Feb. 20–April 20, 1992. Catalogue, with texts by Lynne Cooke, Bice Curiger, and Greg Hilty. Traveled to Kunsthalle Wien, Vienna, Jan. 8–Feb. 28, 1993.

Altonaer Museum in Hamburg, Norddeutches Landesmuseum, *Die Künstlerpostkarte*, March 4–June 8, 1992. Catalogue, with texts by Sabine Blumenröder, Bärbel Hedinger, Gerhard Kaufmann, et al., published by Prestel, Munich. Traveled to Deutsches Postmuseum, Frankfurt, June 30–Sept. 13, 1992.

Kukje Gallery, Seoul, *Words*, April 8–27, 1992. Catalogue, with text by Kyung Mee Park.

Museum Ludwig, Cologne, *Ars Pro Domo*, May 22–Aug. 9, 1992. Catalogue, with texts by Wilfried Dickhoff and Reiner Speck.

Kunstmuseum and Kunsthalle Basel, *Transform: BildObjektSkulptur im 20. Jahrhundert*, June 14–Sept. 27, 1992. Catalogue, with texts by Gottfried Boehm, Eva Keller, Franz Meyer, et al.

Kunst- und Ausstellungshalle der Bundesrepublik Deutschland, Bonn, *Territorium Artis*, June 19–Sept. 20, 1992. Catalogue, with text by Pontus Hulten.

Modernism, San Francisco, *Beyond Just Words*, Sept. 10–Oct. 31, 1992.

Tramway, Glasgow, *Read My Lips: New York AIDS Polemic*, Oct. 26, 1992–Jan. 12, 1993. Catalogue, with text by Simon Watney.

Rhona Hoffman Gallery, Chicago, *Functional Objects by Artists and Architects*, Nov. 20, 1992–Jan. 2, 1993.

1993

Brooke Alexander Editions, New York, *Sculpture and Multiples*, Jan. 8–Feb. 13, 1993.

Whitney Museum of American Art at Champion, Stamford, Connecticut, *The Elusive Object*, Feb. 5–April 14, 1993. Catalogue, with text by Pamela Gruninger Perkins.

The Contemporary Arts Center, Cincinnati, *Mettlesome Meddlesome: Selections from the Collection of Robert J. Shiffler*, Feb. 6–March 20, 1993. Catalogue, with texts by Elaine A. King, Jan Riley, Robert Shiffler, and Marcia Tucker.

Exit Art/The First World, New York, *1920: The Subtlety of Subversion/The Continuity of Intervention*, March 6–April 17, 1993.

Martin-Gropius-Bau, Berlin, *American Art in the Twentieth Century: Painting and Sculpture 1913–1993*, May 8–July 25, 1993. Catalogue, with texts by Brooks Adams, David Anfam, Richard Armstrong, et al. Traveled to Royal Academy of Arts and the Saatchi Gallery, London, Sept. 16–Dec. 12, 1993.

Times Square, New York, *Forty-second Street Art Project 1993*, organized by Creative Time, New York, July 8, 1993–March 1994.

> *Creative Time: Artists Invent, Creative Time Helps Make It Happen* (New York: Creative Time, 1994), pp. 14–19.

Guggenheim Museum SoHo, New York, *Virtual Reality: An Emerging Medium*, Oct. 23–Nov. 1, 1993.

> Karen Whitehouse, "The Museum of the Future," *IEEE Computer Graphics and Applications* (Los Alamitos, Calif.), May 1994, pp. 8–11.

> Jon Ippolito, "Will Virtual Reality Open Doors or Close Them?," *Guggenheim Magazine* 5 (spring–summer 1994), pp. 48–53.

1994

Neuberger Museum, State University of New York at Purchase, *Translucent Writings*, Jan. 30–April 3, 1994. Catalogue, with texts by Robert Adrian, Lucinda H. Gedeon, Grita Insam, Friedrich Kittler, Wolfgang Kos, Ferdinand Schmatz, and Peter Weibel.

Kunsthalle Basel, *Welt-Moral: Moralvorstellungen in der Kunst heute*, April 30–July 31, 1994. Catalogue, with texts by Christoph Grunenberg and Hans Saner.

Sogetsu Plaza, Sogetsu Kaikan, Japan, *Tradition and Invention: Contemporary Artists Interpret the Japanese Garden*, Sept. 1–11, 1994. Catalogue, with texts by Akira Asada and Susan Sontag, published by AmFAR International.

Marieluise Hessel and Richard Black Center for Curatorial Studies and Art in Contemporary Culture, Bard College, Annandale-on-Hudson, New York, *Transformers*, organized by Independent Curators Incorporated, New York, Sept. 21–Nov. 13, 1994. Catalogue, with text by Ralph Rugoff. Traveled to Decker Galleries, Maryland Institute College of Art, Baltimore, Nov. 17–Dec. 17, 1995; Herbert F. Johnson Museum of Art, Cornell University, Ithaca, New York, Jan. 27–March 26, 1996; Nexus Contemporary Art Center, Atlanta, April 12–June 1, 1996; Art Gallery of Windsor, Windsor, Ontario, June 21–Sept. 9, 1996; and Illingworth Kerr Art Gallery of the Alberta College of Art and Design, Calgary, Nov. 4–28, 1996.

Adam Baumgold Fine Art, New York, *Sex*, Oct. 28–Dec. 3, 1994.

Neue Gesellschaft für Bildende Kunst, Berlin, *Gewalt/Geschäfte*, Dec. 10, 1994–Feb. 17, 1995. Catalogue, with texts by Laura Cottingham, Hal Foster, bell hooks, et al.

Institute of Contemporary Arts, London, *The Institute of Cultural Anxiety: Works from the Collection*, Dec. 11, 1994–Feb. 12, 1995. Catalogue, with text by Francis McKee.

Kunstbau Lenbachhaus, Munich, *Rosebud: Jenny Holzer, Matt Mullican, and Lawrence Weiner*, Dec. 14, 1994–Feb. 12, 1995. Catalogue, with texts by Helmut Friedel, Rosa Maria Malet, Michael Tarantino, and Ulrich Wilmes. Traveled to Fundació Joan Miró, Barcelona, Sept. 21–Nov. 26, 1995.

1995

University Art Museum, University of California, Berkeley, *In a Different Light*, Jan. 11–April 9, 1995. Catalogue, with texts by Dan Cameron, Harmony Hammond, Terry Wolverton, et al., published with City Lights Books, San Francisco.

Museum of Modern Art at Heide, Melbourne, *In Five Words or Less*, March 21–May 21, 1995.

Dong-Ah Gallery, Seoul, *Man and Machine: Technology Art*, June 6–July 8, 1995. Catalogue, with text by In Soon Pae.

SITE Santa Fe, *Longing and Belonging: From the Faraway Nearby*, July 14–Oct. 8, 1995. Catalogue, with text by Lon Dubinsky.

The Aspen Art Museum, *Contemporary Drawing: Exploring the Territory*, July 27–Sept. 24, 1995.

The New Museum of Contemporary Art, New York, *Temporarily Possessed: The Semi-Permanent Collection*, Sept. 15–Dec. 17, 1995. Catalogue, with text by Brian Goldfarb, John Hatfield, Laura Trippi, and Mimi Young.

Grande Galerie, Centre Georges Pompidou, Paris, *Fémininmasculin: Le sexe de l'art*, Oct. 24, 1995–Feb. 12, 1996. Catalogue, with texts by Kathy Acker, Bernard Marcadé, Robert Storr, et al.

Center for the Arts, Wesleyan University, Middletown, Connecticut, *Laughter Ten Years After*, Oct. 31–Dec. 9, 1995. Catalogue, with texts by Jo Anna Isaak, Jeanne Silverthorn, and Marcia Tucker. Traveled to Houghton House Gallery, Hobart and William Smith Colleges, Geneva, New York, Feb. 23–April 16, 1996, and Spruance Art Center, Beaver College Art Gallery, Glenside, Pennsylvania, Sept. 16–Oct. 27, 1996.

1996

Athens School of Fine Arts, *Everything That's Interesting Is New: The Dakis Joannou Collection*, organized by The DESTE Foundation for Contemporary Art, Athens, Jan. 20–April 20, 1996. Catalogue, with texts by Jeffrey Deitch and Stuart Morgan. Traveling to Museum of Modern Art, Copenhagen, 1997.

Castello di Rivoli, Museo d'Arte Contemporanea, Turin, *Collezionismo a Torino*, Feb. 15–April 21, 1996. Catalogue, with texts by Gemma De Angelis Testa, Ida Gianelli, Eliana Guglielmi, et al.

Guggenheim Museum SoHo, New York, *Mediascape*, June 14–Sept. 15, 1996. Catalogue, with texts by Annika Blunck, Matthew Drutt, Ursula Frohne, Heinrich Klotz, and Oliver Seifert.

The Museum of Modern Art, New York, *Thinking Print: Books to Billboards, 1980–95*, June 19–Sept. 10, 1996. Catalogue, with text by Deborah Wye.

Musée de Marseille, *Art Embodied*, July 6–Oct. 15, 1996.

Hypobank International S.A., Luxembourg, *Orte des Möglichen—Weibliche Positionen in der zeitgenössischen*

Kunst, Sept. 20–Oct. 20, 1996. Catalogue, with text by Katharina Hegewisch. Traveled to Achenbach Kunsthandel, Düsseldorf, Oct. 25–Nov. 24, 1996.

Florence, *Biennale di Firenze: Il Tempo e la Moda*, Sept. 21–Dec. 15, 1996. Accompanied by xenon projection, Arno river, Sept. 20–22, and texts on taxi hoods throughout the city.

   Virginia Baradel, "Si l'arte sposa la moda: Un esperimento ardito, ma funziona," *Il Mattino di Padova*, Sept. 27, 1996.

   Amy M. Spindler, "When Designers Take Cues from Art," *The New York Times*, Oct. 8, 1996, p. B8.

   Laura Montanari, "Biennale, profumo di sesso," *La Repubblica* (Rome), Oct. 23, 1996.

   Jonathan Turner, "Transporting Truisms," *Artnews* (New York) 96, no. 1 (Jan. 1997), p. 29.

Whitney Museum of American Art, New York, *Views from Abroad: European Perspectives on American Art 2*, organized with Museum für Moderne Kunst, Frankfurt, Oct. 18, 1996–Jan. 5, 1997. Catalogue, with texts by Jean-Christophe Ammann, Mario Kramer, Rolf Lauter, and Adam D. Weinberg. Traveled to Museum für Moderne Kunst, Frankfurt, Jan. 31–May 4, 1997.

Eindhoven, The Netherlands, *Travaux Publics {Public Works}*, organized by Peninsula and Stedelijk Van Abbemuseum, Eindhoven, Dec. 8, 1996–Feb. 9, 1997. Catalogue, with texts by Luk Lambrecht and Tjeu Teeuwen.

SELECTED BIBLIOGRAPHY

Artist's Projects

Artforum (New York) 26, no. 7 (March 1988), p. 116.

Map: Das Papier (New York), no. 4 (summer 1993), unpaginated.

"Lustmord," *Süddeutsche Zeitung Magazin* (Munich), Nov. 19, 1993, pp. 1–31.

   "Drucken mit Blut: Künstlerin vergeudet 90 Liter Lebenssaft," *Berliner Zeitung*, Nov. 12, 1993.

   Fritz Janda, Vera Kettenbach, and Sieglinde Neumann, "Blut: Druck: Der Schock sitzt," *Express Düsseldorf*, Nov. 12, 1993.

   Karl Stankiewitz, "Was darf die Kunst?," *Stuttgarter Nachrichten*, Nov. 13, 1993.

   Hanne Weskott, "Editorial Power and Blood Feuds," *World Art* (Melbourne) 1, no. 1 (Jan. 1994), pp. 10–13.

   David Chandler, "Lustmord," *Creative Camera* (London), no. 336 (Oct.–Nov. 1995), pp. 22–27.

Parkett (Zurich), nos. 40–41 (June 1994).

   Joan Simon, "No Ladders; Snakes: Jenny Holzer's *Lustmord*," *Parkett*, nos. 40–41 (June 1994), pp. 78–97.

Artis (Bern) 48, no. 10 (Oct. 1996), pp. 34–42.

Gerd F. Klein and Thomas Schulte, eds., *The Copylight Book II: An Anthology of Contemporary Design in Three Volumes*. Hamburg: Brainbox, 1996, unpaginated.

By the Artist

A Little Knowledge. New York: self-published, 1979.

"Position Papers" (with Peter Nadin), *Artforum* (New York) 18, no. 6 (Feb. 1980), pp. 29–32.

Black Book. New York: self-published, 1980.

Hotel (with Peter Nadin). New York: Tanam Press, 1980.

Living (with Peter Nadin). New York: self-published, 1980.

Eating Friends (with Peter Nadin). New York: Top Stories, 1981.

Eating Through Living (with Peter Nadin). New York: Tanam Press, 1981.

Truisms and Essays. Halifax: Nova Scotia College of Art and Design Press, 1983.

"Laugh Hard at the Absurdly Evil," in *New Observations*. New York: New Observations and the authors, 1985, pp. 6–7.

Statement, in Katrine Ames, "Why Jane Can't Draw (or Sing, or Dance . . .)," *Newsweek* (New York), special edition, fall–winter 1990, pp. 40–49.

"Eating Friends," in Anne Turyn, ed., *Top Stories*. San Francisco: City Lights Books, 1991, pp. 37–43.

"Laments," in Lou Robinson and Camille Norton, eds., *Resurgent: New Writing by Women*. Chicago: University of Illinois Press, 1992, pp. 216–29.

Statement, in Eric P. Nash, "Does Fashion Matter?," *The New York Times Magazine*, Oct. 24, 1993, pp. 46–72.

Noemi Smolik, ed., *Jenny Holzer: Writing/Schriften*. Stuttgart: Cantz Verlag, 1996.

Interviews with the Artist

Diana Nemiroff, "Personae and Politics: Jenny Holzer," *Vanguard* (Vancouver) 12, no. 9 (Nov. 1983), pp. 26–27.

Jeanne Siegel, "Jenny Holzer's Language Games," *Arts Magazine* (New York) 60, no. 4 (Dec. 1985), pp. 64–68. Reprinted in *Artwords 2: Discourse on the Early 80s*. Ann Arbor, Mich.: UMI Press, 1988, pp. 285–97.

Maralyn Lois Polak, "Jenny Holzer: Messages Are Her Medium," *The Philadelphia Inquirer Magazine*, Sept. 27, 1987, pp. 7–8.

Abigail R. Esman, "Jenny Holzer," *New Art International* (Paris), Feb.–March 1988, pp. 50–53.

Rory MacPherson, "Jenny Holzer," *Splash*, summer 1988, unpaginated.

Steven Evans, "Not All About Death: Jenny Holzer," *Artscribe International* (London), no. 76 (summer 1989), pp. 57–59.

Janine Cirincione, "Activity Can Be Overrated," in Cirincione and Brian D'Amato, eds., *Through the Looking Glass: Artists' First Encounters with Virtual Reality* (exh. cat., Jack Tilton Gallery, New York). Jupiter, Fla.: Softworlds, 1992, pp. 25–29.

Patrick J. B. Flynn, "Jenny Holzer," *The Progressive* (Madison, Wis.) 57, no. 4 (April 1993), pp. 30–34.

Janine Cirincione, "Jenny Holzer Unplugged," *A Gathering of the Tribes* (New York) 3, no. 2 (fall–winter 1993), pp. 10–12.

Barbaralee Diamonstein, "Jenny Holzer, Artist," in Diamonstein, *Inside the Art World: Artists, Directors, Curators, Collectors, Dealers/Conversations with Barbaralee Diamonstein*. New York: Rizzoli, 1994, pp. 107–13.

Burr Snider, "Jenny Holzer: Multidisciplinary Dweeb," *Wired* (San Francisco) 2, no. 2 (Feb. 1994), pp. 76–77.

"Interview with Jenny Holzer," in Allison Moore, ed., *In the Margins: Nineteen Interviews*. Minneapolis: Montgomery Glasoe Fine Art, 1995, pp. 19–21.

Jon Spayde, "What the World Needs Now," *Utne Reader* (Minneapolis) 74, no. 3 (March 1996), pp. 62–77.

On the Artist

Ross Bleckner, "Transcendent Anti-Fetishism," *Artforum* (New York) 17, no. 7 (March 1979), pp. 50–55.

Dan Graham, "Signs," *Artforum* (New York) 19, no. 8 (April 1981), pp. 38–41.

Hal Foster, "Critical Spaces," *Art in America* (New York) 70, no. 3 (March 1982), pp. 115–19.

Benjamin H. D. Buchloh, "Allegorical Procedures: Appropriation and Montage in Contemporary Art," *Artforum* (New York) 21, no. 10 (Sept. 1982), pp. 43–56.

Hal Foster, "Subversive Signs," *Art in America* (New York) 70, no. 10 (Nov. 1982), pp. 88–92.

Carter Ratcliff, "Jenny Holzer," *The Print Collector's Newsletter* (New York) 13, no. 5 (Nov.–Dec. 1982), pp. 149–52.

Fredric Jameson, "Postmodernism and Consumer Society," in Hal Foster, ed., *The Anti-Aesthetic: Essays on Postmodern Culture*. Port Townsend, Wash.: Bay Press, 1983, pp. 111–25.

Donald Kuspit, "Gallery Leftism," *Vanguard* (Vancouver) 12, no. 9 (Nov. 1983), pp. 22–25.

Craig Owens, "The Discourse of Others: Feminists and Postmodernism," in Hal Foster, ed., *The Anti-Aesthetic: Essays on Postmodern Culture*. Port Townsend, Wash.: Bay Press, 1983, pp. 57–77.

Paul Smith, "Difference in America," *Art in America* (New York) 73, no. 4 (April 1985), pp. 190–99.

Russell Bowman, "Words and Images: A Persistent Paradox," *Art Journal* (New York) 45, no. 4 (winter 1985), pp. 335–43.

Ellen Handy, "Notes on Criticism: Art and Transactionalism," *Arts Magazine* (New York) 61, no. 2 (Oct. 1986), pp. 48–53.

Jean-Pierre Bordaz, "Jenny Holzer and the Spectacle of Communication," *Parkett* (Zurich), no. 13 (1987), pp. 30–33.

Donald Kuspit, "Regressive Reproduction and Throwaway Conscience," *Artscribe International* (London), no. 61 (Jan.–Feb. 1987), pp. 26–31. Reprinted

in *The New Subjectivism: Art in the 1980s*. Ann Arbor, Mich.: UMI Press, 1988, pp. 407–15.

Margaret Hawkins, "Jenny Holzer's Abstract Messages Are Signs of the Times," *Chicago Sun-Times*, Feb. 27, 1987, p. 52.

Dan Cameron, "Post-Feminism," *Flash Art* (Milan), no. 132 (Feb.–March 1987), pp. 80–83.

David Bonetti, "What's in a Word? Jenny Holzer's Message Is the Medium," *The Boston Phoenix*, Oct. 16, 1987, Section 3, pp. 4–5.

John Howell, "Jenny Holzer: The Message Is the Medium," *Artnews* (New York) 87, no. 6 (summer 1988), pp. 122–27.

Michael Brenson, "Media Artist Named to Represent U.S. at '90 Venice Biennale," *The New York Times*, July 27, 1988, pp. C15, C17.

———, "Jenny Holzer: The Message Is the Message," *The New York Times*, Aug. 7, 1988, pp. H29, H35.

Patrick Kurp, "Visual Artist's Way with Words Leads to Her Venice Biennale," *Sunday Times Union* (Albany, N.Y.), Aug. 14, 1988, p. G5.

Kay Larson, "Signs of the Times: Jenny Holzer's Art Words Catch On," *New York Magazine*, Sept. 5, 1988, pp. 49–53.

Torene Svitil, "Jenny Holzer," *Exposure* (Los Angeles), Sept.–Oct. 1988, pp. 42–43.

Lawrence Chua, "Jenny Holzer: Holzer, Like Burroughs, Couches Subversion in Seeming Nonsense," *Flash Art* (Milan), no. 142 (Oct. 1988), pp. 112–13.

Paul Taylor, "Jenny Holzer Sees Aphorism as Art," *Vogue* (New York), Nov. 1988, pp. 388–93, 456.

Sarah Kent, "Jenny Holzer: Signs of the Times," *Time Out* (London), Nov. 30, 1988, pp. 26–27.

Mary Anne Staniszewski, "Jenny Holzer: Language Communicates," *Flash Art* (Milan), no. 143 (Nov.–Dec. 1988), p. 112.

Louisa Buck, "Word Play," *The Face* (London), Dec. 1988, pp. 128–31.

James Danziger, "American Graffiti," *The Sunday Times Magazine* (London), Dec. 4, 1988, p. 5.

Louisa Buck, "Clean and Keen, Clean and Mean," *The Guardian* (London), Dec. 14, 1988, p. 17.

Sarah Craddock, "In the End Was the Word," *Weekend Guardian* (London), Jan. 14, 1989, p. 21.

Karin Lipson, "The Message Is Her Medium," *New York Newsday*, March 19, 1989, Part II, pp. 13–15.

Vikki Michalski, "Call It What You Want, It's Art," *Lancaster Eagle Gazette*, June 11, 1989, p. C8.

Eleanor Heartney, "The New Social Sculpture," *Sculpture* (Washington, D. C.) 8, no. 4 (July–Aug. 1989), pp. 24–27.

John Carlin, "80's Art Chart," *Paper* (New York) 6, no. 12 (Dec. 1989–Jan. 1990), pp. 62–63.

Eleanor Heartney, "Jenny Holzer," in Sue Taylor, ed., *The Refco Collection*. Chicago: The Refco Group, 1990, pp. 74–75.

"Jenny Holzer," in Charles Moritz, ed., *Current Biography Yearbook 1990*. New York: H. W. Wilson Company, 1990, pp. 305–09.

James Lewis, "Powers of Disingenuousness," *Art Issues* (Los Angeles), no. 11 (May 1990), pp. 13–17.

Gianfranco Mantegna, "Parole per la vita," *Chorus* (Milan) 1, no. 5 (June 1990), pp. 38–40.

Edward M. Gomez, "Quarreling over Quality," *Time* (New York), special edition, fall 1990, pp. 61–62.

Peter Bellamy, *The Artist Project: Portraits of the Real Art World/New York Artists 1981–1990*. New York: IN Publishing, 1991, p. 108.

Yoshiharu Suenobu, "Jenny Holzer," *Marie Claire* (Tokyo), no. 88 (1991), pp. 332–33.

Nicholas Zurbrugg, "Jenny Holzer," *Eyeline: East Coast Contemporary Visual Arts* (Brisbane), no. 16 (spring 1991), pp. 18–21.

John Howell, "Contemporary Art and the Pursuit of Perfection in the House of Asher," *Elle Decor* (New York) 2, no. 6 (Aug. 1991), p. 61.

Elizabeth Hayt-Atkins, "It's Art by Fax and by Phone," *Elle Decor* (New York) 2, no. 8 (Oct. 1991), pp. 42–44.

"Women on Men: The Uneasy State of Masculinity Now," *Esquire* (New York) 116, no. 4 (Oct. 1991), p. 144.

Evelyn Schels, "Jenny Holzer: Meisterin der Sprüche," *Elle* (Munich) 1, no. 11 (Nov. 1991), pp. 304–06.

Michael Auping, *Jenny Holzer.* Universe Series on Women Artists. New York: Universe Publishing, 1992.

Leanne Boepple, "Stone for Art's Sake," *Stone World* (Syracuse, N.Y.) 9, no. 3 (March 1992), pp. 46–52, 89.

Steve Gabarino, "Going Against Type," *Entertainment Weekly* (New York), special issue, May 8, 1992, p. 10.

Susan Dyer, "The Sibyl Cave Revisited: Jenny Holzer," *Women's Art Magazine* (London), no. 46 (May–June 1992), pp. 18–19.

Yvette van Caldenborgh, *Made in the U.S.A.* (exh. cat.). Rotterdam: Caldic Collection, 1993.

Robert Hughes, "The View from Piccadilly," *Time* (New York), Oct. 4, 1993, pp. 78–79.

Art of This Century: The Guggenheim Museum and Its Collection. New York: Guggenheim Museum, 1993, pp. 303–07.

Liz McQuiston, *Graphic Agitation: Social and Political Graphics since the Sixties.* London: Phaidon Press, 1993, pp. 28–29, 46, 116.

Roland Hagenberg, "Jenny, der fels," *Vogue* (Munich), no. 1 (Jan. 1994), pp. 188–93.

Richard Lacayo, "If Everyone Is Hip . . . Is Anyone Hip?," *Time* (international edition), Aug. 8, 1994, pp. 34–39.

Dora Bassi, "Autoritratti multimediali: Il fervore profetico di Jenny Holzer," *Lapis* (Milan), no. 23 (Sept. 1994), pp. 48–49.

Susanne Lingemann, "7 starke Frauen in New York," *Art* (Hamburg), no. 12 (Dec. 1994), pp. 16–19.

Sabine Dylla, "Jenny Holzer: 'Pure Writing' Als Plastische Form," in *Jahrbuch '95: Institut für moderne Kunst Nürnberg.* Nuremberg: Verlag für Moderne Kunst Nürnberg, 1995, pp. 44–53.

Yvette van Caldenborgh and J. N. A. van Caldenborgh, *A Collection Sculptures* (exh. cat.). Rotterdam: Caldic Collection, 1995.

Michael Sand, "Who's Afraid of Cyberspace," *Tate: The Art Magazine* (London), no. 6 (summer 1995), pp. 36–39.

Marilyn Berlin Snell, "The Familiar Face of Fascism," *Utne Reader* (Minneapolis) 72, no. 10 (Nov.–Dec. 1995), pp. 5, 54–59.

David Seidner, *The Face of Contemporary Art.* Munich: Gina Kehayoff, 1996, p. 12.

"Entschlossene 50: Frauen für die Cosmo-Aktion," *Cosmopolitan* (Munich), no. 3 (March 1996), pp. 62–63.

Sascha Hehn, "Reigh beschenkt: Wie einen das leben verwöhnen kann," *Süddeutsche Zeitung Magazin* (Munich), Nov. 22, 1996, pp. 72–73.

Anneliese Zwez, "Bad Girls und Prinzessinnen im Elfenbeinturm," *Fraz: Frauezitig,* no. 4 (Dec. 1996–Feb. 1997), pp. 27–29.

Photo Credits

All photos courtesy of Jenny Holzer and Barbara Gladstone Gallery, New York, unless otherwise noted. For full copyright information, contact the photographers or institutions listed below.

cover, pp. 38, 53: Thomas Holder; back cover: Attilio Maranzano; pp. 9–11, 128: David Heald, Guggenheim Museum; pp. 16, 102–03: Salvatore Licitra; p. 30: John Deane; pp. 45, 62, 69–70, 81: Jenny Holzer; pp. 46–47: Patricia Blake; pp. 48–51, 84: ©Lisa Kahane; pp. 54, 85: Edward Klamm; p. 58: Paul Wrede; p. 59: Tom Loonan, courtesy of Albright-Knox Art Gallery, Buffalo; pp. 60–61: Maggie Hopp; p. 68: Deborah Oglesby; p. 74: Larry Lame; pp. 75, 100: Glenn Halvorson; p. 77: Pelka/Noble, New York; p. 78: M. Michalski; pp. 82–83: Cosimo di Leo Ricatto; p. 86: Michael Tropea; p. 88: Rudolf Wakonigg; p. 89: Friedrich Meschede; pp. 90, 96–99: Michael Agee; p. 95: Bill Jacobson, courtesy of Dia Center for the Arts, New York; p. 104: Bernhard Schaub; pp. 106, 108–09: Nic Tenwiggenhorn; p. 107: Martin Köttering; p. 110: Shigeo Anzai; p. 114: Edward Addeo; pp. 115–17: Alan Richardson; pp. 118–19: Werner Lieberknecht, ©Kunstmuseum des Kantons Thurgau, Kartause Ittingen, Warth, Switzerland; pp. 120–21: Hans-Dieter Kluge, ©Förderkreis der Leipziger Galerie für Zeitgenössische Kunst, Leipzig, Germany; pp. 122, 124–25: Christian Wachter.

Jenny Holzer wishes to thank the following for their assistance with photography: Abteilung Kultur und Wissenschaft des Amtes der Niederösterreichischen Landesregierung, Erlauf, Austria; The Artangel Trust, London; Artspace, San Francisco; Center for Contemporary Art, Ujazdowski Castle, Warsaw; Contemporary Art Center, Art Tower Mito, Mito, Japan; The Corcoran Gallery of Art, Washington, D.C.; Creative Time, New York; Förderkreis der Leipziger Galerie für Zeitgenössische Kunst, Leipzig, Germany; Rhona Hoffman Gallery, Chicago; Kunstmuseum des Kantons Thurgau, Kartause Ittingen, Warth, Switzerland; Lower Manhattan Cultural Council, New York; Nevada Institute for Contemporary Art, University of Nevada, Las Vegas; Public Art Fund, Inc., New York; Seattle Art Museum; Monika Sprüth Galerie, Cologne; Städtische Galerie, Nordhorn, Germany; Walker Art Center, Minneapolis; Westfälisches Landesmuseum für Kunst und Kulturgeschichte, Münster; and Williams College Museum of Art, Williamstown, Massachusetts.